Praise for

All Roads Lead from Massilia

These short excursions into the many Frances Philip Kobylarz knows and loves are complete in themselves and add up to one traveler's intelligent, visceral, immediate appreciation of French culture. A tonic getaway for the weary and jaded, this is both a cheap vacation, and a rich one. I loved it. *All Roads Lead from Massilia* is engrossing and palpable.

~ Stephen D. Gutierrez, author of *The Mexican Man in His Backyard, Stories & Essays*

This is not a collection.
This is an arsenal.
An arsenal of rhetorical daggers.
Daggers stabbing straight at the heart – of truth itself.

~ Eric Michael Moberg, author of *Big Noise at the Funky Butt Jass Club* and *Most Dangerous Man*

All Roads Lead from Massilia takes readers on a journey through geographical, cultural, and emotional landscapes in a hologram of words that reveal the ghosts of France while rooted to American comparisons Kobylarz so desperately tries to unroot. Kobylarz creates Baudrillard's America in reverse with his vignettes of wandering the streets and sewers of Paris, or his rural span of the French countryside and the people who inhabit them on the surface and down below.

~ Kerry Hillis Goff, author of *When the Haunted are Favored*

Kobylarz's reflections on terraces, baked delicacies, Cézanne, the essence of walls, the erotic life, poverty and Super Gluing one's shoes, French doors, the hazards of solitude, café contemplation, hiking, the birth echo of caves with "crystals like immediate stars," leave the reader with the overall absorbed sensuality and meteorology of the landscape remaining, against most odds, among the lasting values of a sane, enthusiastic, contemplative life-affirming sensibility.

~ Doren Robbins, author of *Twin Extra, Amnesty Muse* and *Parking Lot Mood Swing*

. . . à Marseille les gens sont secrets et durs.
Dieu, que cette ville est difficile!
        Blaise Cendrars. L'Homme Foudroyé.
        Paris: Gallimard, 1973. Editions Denoël.

preemptory NOTE:
Lazarus lived 30 years after his resurrection–
        le 31 august 63 a.d. – died (?) in Marseille.

This book serves as an installment in the
discursive triptych begun by Zbigniew Herbert's
A Barbarian in the Garden and continued
by Jean Baudrillard's *America.*

All Roads Lead from Massilia

Philip Kobylarz

EVERYTIME PRESS

Everytime
Press

ISBN: 978-1-925536-27-0

Everytime Press
4 Warburton Street
Magill SA 5072
Australia

Email: sales@everytimepress.com
Website: http://www.everytimepress.com
Everytime Press catalogue: http://www.everytimepress.com/apps/webstore/

Front cover photograph © Marc Field
Author, back cover and interior photographs © Philip Kobylarz
Cover design © Matt Potter

Also available as an eBook
ISBN: 978-1-925536-28-7

to

Wiktoria, Loretta, Victoria, Karina,
Kodiak, Szoltan, & Gitane and
even Monique

CONTENTS

ARRIVAL

The airport is crowded, voice from overhead, louder than necessary, singing phrases that cannot be understood, except for the names of places: Amsterdam, Rabat, Stuttgart, Algiers, Madrid, Paris, Dakar. It could be an airport in any major city in the world, yet there are subtleties of difference/definition. Near the bathroom, a woman waits seated at a table, furniture dated by a once modern aerospace style: mid rocket years sixties. She has what appears to be an ashtray barely filled with coins in front of her. She is not smoking. Sometimes, she opens her paperback and takes a glance. Mostly, she sits staring vacantly into the distance, not even hearing the toilettes flushing behind her, the dull murmur of plumbing constantly cleansing itself. She is waiting for a tip, for a few coins that the release from a bodily function is worth these days. Usually not much, a franc or two. Never a paper bill. Never too much.

It is time to catch the connecting flight. Nearly a half an hour before it is to take off, passengers are queuing for seats. The line, at first modeled loosely on the British form – straight with ample elbow room – soon, as the countdown begins, erodes into a flimsy semi-circle. The intelligent, spawns of a survival of the fittest process, begin to sneak in on either side of the semi-circle, towards the entrance gate. White-haired men are seen zipping small dogs into carry-on bags, not taking the time to make sure they don't catch the dog's curly hair in the seam. Copies of *Le*

13

Monde or *Le Provençal* are hastily tucked under arm. The concept of personal space is all but obliterated: people stand on each other's heels, elbows connect with sides; humid after meal breath is shared, anonymous line-standers become almost intimate with one another, scents of perfume are exchanged, yet no one is pushed to the point of painful discomfort or even the threshold of anger. This is just the way the machine works. Conversation about the weather and the ineptitude of airline personnel breaks out sporadically. Cigarettes are extinguished at the last breath, the last second. Through a cloud of exhaled tobacco, you enter France.

TANGENTIAL

Escape the confusion of flight numbers that add up to their own trigonometry with no solutions and slip into the city that is much too far from the airport. The fields that surround are flat and mildly undulating, as fields should be, a haze hangs over them to suggest the mystery that lies beyond. On the bus into the city, the people are well-dressed and as silent as mutes. Passing through over- and underpasses, then into the preliminary maze of the outskirts, trash of a different nature lines the road side. Occasionally, there are pieces of habitations: light fixtures, fenders of outdated automobiles, racks from refrigerators, lampshades, then paper refuse of products that a third world country can only dream of: brightly colored garbage as decoration. This country, like other fantastically rich countries, has too much to throw away.

The body heat within the bus fogs the windows, obscuring views of places that don't want to be seen anyway. The silence on the bus is reverence for the hard, lonely work of travel.

ENTER THE LABYRINTH

*Maintenant tu marches dans Paris tout seul
parmi la foule/ Des troupeaux d'autobus
mugissants près de toi roulent/ L'angoisse de
l'amour te serre le gosier/ Comme si tu ne
devais jamais plus être aimé*

Apollinaire

Paris is a monument to itself. A monument constantly building and rebuilding its own glory. Its busiest and most remarkable streets, Boulevard St. Michel, Saint Germain des Prés, are filled with steady lines of people skirting around crews of road repair men. The bowels of the street are exposed for all to see. Rubble, dirt, rocks, why plaster of Paris is named so. Pipes coming from and returning to their respective circles of hell. Absent is the smell, feel, texture of asphalt: here the streets and the buildings are, for the most part, real. Made of the stuff that they have always been made of. Made of concrete, stone, marble, dirt, materials that the sense of touch desires. This is no Michigan Avenue where the monstrosities that surround are of unimaginable glass and steel welded together into canyons of inhumanity that mock nature. Trees here aren't belittled by their surroundings, they are, within the realms of their little wrought iron fences, an integral part of the city. Bird apartments. Parks, within the city, crop up unexpectedly and offer a refuge of

16

vegetation and real earth underfoot. They are also gathering places for those seeking refuge within refuge: people *peuple* them – reading books, lovers sit on each other's lap inspecting their reflection in each other's eyes, the homeless sleep on their benches undisturbed, pigeons decorate them as if they are about to break into a game of pétanque. They aren't the tools for guided amusement, swings, seesaws, as they are in the States. Here, their inhabitants know what to do in city parks: breathe, relax, sit, see, be. Do absolutely nothing.

The apartment buildings that surround these green spaces, are, on a human scale, gigantic. Rows and rows of shutters, mostly closed, but in the months of summer, wide open. They reveal backdrops of horrendous wallpaper, beautiful antique armoires or bureaus, lines of laundry hanging from tiny perches of porches, odd light fixtures retained due to function more than aesthetic. The oddest aspect: there are millions of these decorated caves, filled with strange and wonderful people who have not opted for life in the new American-style suburbs that unfortunately exist, those who cling to the myth of the city and populate it with their belief in the grandiosity of it all. The rents, apparent to all from pastings in windows of real estate agents (as if they were a type of coveted pastry), are explosively high. Apartments with terraces, or at least, rooms of differing levels, are worth a child's weight in silver. The views from them garner every penny spent. Seen from within the city, the city reveals its very brainwork, its interior, clockwork of its architecture, an exploded inside view. Inhabitants bear with the impossible task of parking, the crowded metros, grocery stores packed with hungry rummagers at a preordained shopping time, just to live the monuments of their lives in a monument to life: the greatest city ever achieved.

STREETS

Appropriately called rues, they contain a certain sadness, the kind embodied in great works of art. The Mona Lisa's plaintive smile, the gloom of Redon's etchings color these traverses and alleys. The bizarrity of Atget's project comes into light. Why a man would spend a lifetime photographing block after block of mere passageways and buildings becomes clear only upon visitation of the scene. The beauty of the city's arterial street system often escapes a black and white, matter of fact real time presentation. The immense layering of humanity is lost, unless stumbled upon, followed within. Around every corner, a new discovery is to be made.

Kiosks stand like obelisks centering a place or pinpointing a corner. Covered in a skin of past and present events, they molt themselves of happenings: concerts, lectures, circuses, calls for auditions, ways in which to assimilate deeper into the buildings and life that surrounds. More numerous than their sheets of glossy sheaves are the millions of staples sunk into their wooden planks, like eyeteeth multiplying. One cannot pass a kiosk without looking at it, or touching. They are the un-peopled sentries of the streets patiently waiting to ring out the news for those who have the time, or interest, to connect. They are polyglots, offering conversation in Vietnamese, English, Arabic, Russian, incorrect French. They repel with their banal vulgarity: the telephone sex number of a posing half-nude named Yaya or

Mimi revealing a flank of thigh and two crescents of nipples. This is most naturally pasted next to a multi-color poster of a coming concert of Rimski-Korsakov. Two sides of the same coin in the city of any desire.

Another trinket of the past that characterizes the interior – *pissoires*. Not the automated pay toilets that look like construction worker johns on the moon, but green-painted metal mock Calders that stand as drones. Private pillboxes. What these are actually needed for can't be simply explained. A man here hasn't the slightest hesitation in pulling his vehicle over to the side of the road and pissing one step from his car door. Or, as a pedestrian, beelining to the nearest bush or semi-darkened doorway, to relieve himself in a stream of eternity. They must serve as relics of medieval days, when walkways served as sewers; or perhaps reminders of the war: singular Maginot lines, tiny bunkers unto themselves, where the army of quotidian life can enter a coat of armor, peer through the small window-holes, and release a singular cannon with hardly even having to aim. In the months of summer, the *pissoires* add to the humid flavor of the streets, adding a different brand of stench to the air, which is characteristically unlike the bad water aftertaste of New York's waterfront or the smell within the drained swamp skyscraper park on either side of the Chicago River. The structures are painted green – to suggest vegetation? To be inconspicuous? Whatever the motive, their existence in scent and color says it all.

LANDSCAPE

Countryside. That which is outside of city, undulating planes of green, stands of trees, is, by suggestion, portrayed accurately in clouds of daybreak, sunset. In this city that dazzles the eye with its multifold inventions and re-inventions of architecture, the sky hangs unnoticed. Rarely is there enough empty space to tempt a viewer to look up. A crook in the neck from walking too much in one day will do. Above, shape shifters: white, grey, backgrounds of pink, yellow, or the usual blue.

What is particular about Paris is the ornamentation it provides for its already remarkable river Seine. Nowhere in America is there a river so brazenly decorated. Not even along its sister the Mississippi. No New Orleans, Memphis, or Minneapolis celebrates its arterial flow as the quays, the embankments, the islands of Paris do. The result of this appreciation of water as destination is found in the annoying bateaux-mouches that light up the night-time flow, and encase buildings in spotlights, as if they are in the process of mining for tourist attractions. In the U.S., there are riverboat cruises on historical paddle boats, but the focus of these trips is to internalize the pleasures of the river's freedom by providing such distractions as "fine" dining and low stakes gambling. In Paris, to see the city from a boat is to become a platelet within the blood flow. The *Ile de la Cité* is a microcosm of the metaphor of Paris: encircled by placidity, a structure of greatness, of pomp, residing to mark the spot of a coming together and resting and realization that you are somewhere and the resulting beauty of it and of your realization. Celtic tribes. Romans. Their descendants. Invading barbarians. A mingling of a certain Gallic jumble of it all.

The larger parks of the city are sculpted, mainly by the years and ensuing history, into gathering places somewhere in between civilization and the wild. There are hardly any momentous forms of nature, although some buttes do remain, and in the places of loping hills, kept and unkempt gardens, lawns of sensuous grass, man's attempt to comment upon, invade, or tame these oases is ever-present. That the word butte, used in the American West to ordinate square erosional plugs of mountains, comes from the French word to describe a hill built to absorb target-shot bullets: *butte de tir, but:* goal. But in America we've already killed nature off enough so we rifle highway signs. Deconstruction of the final metaphor. Manifest Density.

Here, hills have a Zen-like quality and style: Romanesque columns rise from a pond, Italianate bridges hop a stream, triumphal arches erode among husks of tree trunks years older than their manmade partners. Something like the contemplative quality of the monument park in Washington D.C. with its Japanese cherries and Greek revival architecture, a tranquil zone like this is usually overlooked as a non-walkable banality. But then that capitol was designed by a Frenchman. In eternal balance: humanity's dual nature; one angelic, one wild; as represented in the plans these parks carve out of the earth, the rocks, the vegetal consciousness that is already there. And will be after we are long gone.

Sewers of pariS

Are underground; the glory underneath the glory. Filled with the bones of Egyptians, of captured mummies, of broken, stolen obelisks. They contain stashes of great art hidden by departing Nazis. Reenactments of Roman catacombs, with buried treasures, vases, statuettes, wall paintings done by nomadic Etruscans. Are the bowels of the city filtering the spore-filled waste of the world's best food and wine, processed into bile, a rich pâté of fertilizer. Are built with the monoliths of druids. Concentrically circle the great town leading down to a Plutonic cesspool of regeneration. Provide getaways for the *Wanted*, including the cave-like abode Jack the Ripper inhabited in his last, miserable, rat-like years of existence. Lead to secret bunkers where the armies of France, and her many Kings and Emperors concealed treasures earned in victory: golden samovars, a jade-studded crown of a caliph, the first horologe (made of silver and ivory), an original copy, in gold leaf and camel leather, of the Koran.

DeparturE

Rue Haute-des-Ursins. Impasse des Provençaux. Rue Beurrière. Rue Jacinthe. Place d'Enfer. Have all disappeared, physically, or by name. In this city, streets, through history, have acted as revolving doors. They have been built upon, or continued into different places from the ones they had once been. Their existences have been recorded in photographs (see Atget and Marville) and literature: Henry Miller, Orwell, Baudelaire, to mention three drops in the bucket. More so than the monuments of Invalides or Notre-Dame, the Dome of Sacré Coeur, the myth of the Left Bank, the streets of Paris will tempt you to return.

Even though you can still go to the cobbled streets of Montmartre and find an enclosed square of artists painting landscapes and portraits, artists who will take your seventy dollars (conveniently located on the square is a money changing office) and after they share some words with you in English, Italian, or German, will head into the local bar to make good on a tab, or begin another. Art eternally inspiring itself.

Even though you can still amble through the city to the gate of Père Lachaise and get lost in the city within a city of tombs and hauntingly beautiful burial sites and, at the grave of Chopin or Apollinaire, find freshly cut flowers and people in silence, in awe, visiting, paying respects, this will serve as an experience enough to never be repeated.

Even though you can play tourist and visit the horrendous Beaubourg, escalating up its tubular exoskeleton to find a joke of an eatery at the top with food priced as if there were a siege taking place below, yet beyond it, a spectacular view of the city in mid-afternoon haze, with domes and spires silhouetting the beyond as an invitation to try and find, within the maze, their buried foundations, you will snap a few photos, stand spellbound at its entrance square, upon departure, to watch the few odd street musicians play their tunes, juggle bowling pins, or preach about the end of the world. And the invention of others.

Always awaiting are the streets, the one true glory of the city, to take you back to your hotel, in style, with enchantment, flowing with ever-present water and the rags of the *cantonnier* in the gutters, alive with refuse, empty wine bottles, spit, the footfalls of millions of people like you who came here to find the secret of Paris, who unknowingly cross over it, step upon it, drive through it, for eternity, everyday. City of lights. No, city of rues.

AFTERTHOUGHT

So many things not done, so much not seen. So many shops not penetrated because the shop owners follow the customers around and reproach them for touching the merchandise. Having only walked through the Pigalle district in amazement of neon and music muffled by the dark halls that contained sounds. Having not the courage, or the will, to pay the feeble price of admission that it costs to enter one of the "show boxes" in the middle of the street to see the one dancing girl dance her interpretation of the dance of seven veils. Having not attempted the Louvre or the Musée d'Orsay because there was so much to see outside of these giant reliquaries, living museums of sight, smell, ambulance wails, storefronts reflecting desire, the women, the men overdressed to compete with their more lovely rivals, the Roman amphitheater where men, high on smoke, were playing serious boules, the lovers in the metro melting into one another. Seduced, as is not the case in any American city, perhaps any other city in the world, to come back for more.

MANNERISMS

The rudeness of the French is a deep ingrained cliché. It occurs mainly in Paris, in the summer, during the height of tourist season. Remember, many of the stores aren't air conditioned and the humidity can be unbearable. If you don't attempt to use the few phrases of the language that you've retained from college or high school, it will only worsen the dispute over the café bill. Patience is not something valued in this culture, although it is dearly needed in day-to-day life. France is a country that can be put to a standstill by its citizens. Mail and bus strikes occur, especially in the case of the latter, much too frequently.

The refuge from this matter of fact gruffness can be found occurring at any latitude south, say of Lyon. The south of France is another country, another state of mind and being. Enter civilization at its best.

On y sent je ne sais quoi d'oriental. Marseille est maintenant ce que devait être la Perse dans l'Antiquité, Alexandrie au Moyen Age: un capharnaüm, une Babel de toutes nations, où l'on voit des cheveux blonds, ras, de grandes barbes noires, la peau blanche rayée de veines bleues, le teint olivâtre de L'Asie, des yeux bleus, des regards noirs, tous les costumes, la veste, le manteau, le drap, la toile, la colerette rabattue des Anglais, le turban et les larges pantalons des Turcs.

Gustave Flaubert, *Notes de Voyages*, 1910

Marseilles is hot and loud. They scream the newspapers and all the shops seem full of caged birds, parrots and canaries, shrieking too.

Mansfield, Katherine
Letters to John Middleton Murry
London: Constable & Co. Ltd., 1951.

SECOND CITY

As the landscape shifts from a northerly lay of fields and hills to a more dramatic, weathered, arid, mountainous south, so the people change. Life, in fields, farmhouses, stretches of rivers and their wild quais of trees and stone escarpment, gains vividness. The sun is essential, a bright yellow, or whiteness, either way an invisible bleaching agent. Whereas the Rocky Mountains are formidable, wild, and barren of human meddling while stretching in vistas of foreverness, the Alps, not technically as expansive, are more condensed, like rows upon rows of shark teeth, rising to snow-covered peaks and resplendent in carpets of vegetation. Snowstorms in July and August are not as rare as some would wish. These peaks outline the border with Italy like a running tear in between heaven and ground.

This rugged country, one senses, is the prototype for the ghost of the idea that continues to haunt the world: the dream of a West, myth America, land of cowboys, men and women somewhat at odds with, yet symbiotic in a wildly beautiful landscape forever evading the taming forces of civilization.

In the American West, one suspects that the pioneers' journey across the region was of such a hardship that the cities settled, and left to prosper, or die out into ghost towns, are mostly in basins or meadow lands in between ranges. Phoenix, Los Angeles, Las Vegas, Denver. In France, the cities, more so, villages, are built into the sides of the mountains as an integral part of the land/humanscape. In a city of the U.S. west, take even Alburquerque or Boise or Salt Lake City for example, you find yourself in civilization among, under, surrounded by mountains. In Montpellier, Marseille, or Annecy, you are within the nature that surrounds; in the case of the first, you're on top of it. In the U.S., one can search for the lay of the land, the junction of the city to its environment; in southern France, you are constantly a part of its topography.

Perhaps that is why Provence is known as that, a province. Once a branch of Roman colonization, it remains marked so not only by name. But what is it a province of? It no longer belongs to Caesar. Its citizens range from wealthy Britons to *Pieds Noirs* to fruit merchants from Tunisia and Morocco to generations of Provençaux. The people of this region are decidedly not one thing: Parisian. This can be easily discovered by driving around the area in a rental car with Paris plates; locals tell you where and where not to park, police comment on the style of your driving, clearly a tension exists between the southerners and those of the capital city.

Just as Paris is host to the world in the summer, the south of France is host to all of its other regions when it is vacation time. Those who know where to go, go south. Among the numerous amenities it has to offer are sunlight, sea, escape.

Considering the southeast, it is a place unparalleled by nowhere in the U.S. Monterey Bay and mid to lower California are similar in landforms, aridity, but the Californias are elongated in comparison and the flora is of a less resplendent variety. The vegetation of the desert southwest crops up in Provence, as mountains and farm land of Appalachia are suggested. The most captivating aspect about this area of France is its diversity. One would have to drive hours, even days, to experience the different formations, plant life, no-man's-lands, and outposts of humanity that this part of the country has within the area of the state of Maine. It is a province of those who have adopted it in their heart as a sacred place, to visit, take in, be a part of, however briefly, or however infinite. It is an infinitude of variety. Words offer it little compliment.

The Neanderthals knew. The Ligurians knew. The Greeks knew. The Romans knew. The Provençal poets knew. The Saracens and the Moors knew. Unfortunately, the rich and famous knew, thereby spoiling the Côte d'Azur with money. The Impressionists knew. All of France knows. All of Europe knows. The world knows. I knew but I didn't believe it, couldn't believe it, until I arrived.

PorT

Anges frais débarqués à Marseille hier matin
Apollinaire, Guillaume. Alcools.
Paris: Gallimard, 1966.

Marseille is the other capital of France. It's the second largest city (although Lyon with its suburbs is more populous), serving as the Los Angeles of the country. But it is an L.A. that is intimate with the sea and surrounding mountains because it is entrapped between the two with hardly any escape routes. The mountains that surround it are eerily as white as snow, and banded by black lines of water erosion and strips of green vegetation. The forest that clings to the hills is of innumerable types of flowering scrub, pine, and vegetation characteristic of maritime climates and is brazenly Mediterranean. The *arbouse* tree sprouts red spiky fruits that can be eaten. Giant white mushrooms looking like polished calcite unearth mattresses of pine needles. The topography is miraculous: cliffs that overhang the changing green/blue/turquoise Mediterranean, plains and fields of farmland, craggy outcrops, a landscape wilder than any inhabited area of the Wild West.

But she has a bad reputation. This is a good thing. It keeps the frail of mind away. It's true that the city has a diverse population including many "Arabs": immigrants from North

Africa; a thriving community of Vietnamese, Armenians, Greeks, of course Italians and Spaniards, probably thousands of other ethnicities. The racial tension, albeit present, is merely an undercurrent that rarely rears its ugly head. One can walk a few streets off the *Canebière,* the main downtown drag, and be in a Casbah-like bazaar of fish, fruits, clothes, many kinds of valuable and worthless items on sale, with the voices of the merchants haranguing, a crowd of shoppers nose to neck, to get a taste of the mythical East.

The North African population inhabits a large part of the city's north district. They seem to keep to themselves, but the younger generations have wholeheartedly embraced Western-ism: in the clothes they wear, in a capitalistic attitude towards self-gain, in raï and rap music. From personal experience, let it be stated that never an incident of unfriendliness has occurred or been observed. Once, while taking an afternoon stroll through New York's Washington Square, I thought my life was in danger. The States thrive on random confrontation/violence. It's foolish to believe the myths recorded in literature (including travel writing) or those propounded by Hollywood. The streets of Marseille can be walked at any time of the day or night without worry and with as much caution as anyone would walk any big city. There are borders, but they are penetrable.

The North Africans have borne the brunt of racism in southern France, most immediately stemming from Le Pen and *Le Front National.* On the cultural front, even the generation of writers whose parents came from Algeria or other North African countries, seem to have an invisible wall to contend with. Their literature, called *Beur,* is considered by most academic institutions as Francophone literature – written in French, about the experience of living in France, yet somehow not exactly French. It may be a blessing in disguise in the sense of it being a way to set apart their collective experience, in creating something new and different which requires a special sensitivity. Yet such classifications bespeak of a kind of border drawing that leaves one with a certain unease.

So among the chic, dressed in black, high-heeled women, the slickly attired men in Italian shoes and leather jackets, turbans and skull caps can be seen. On closer inspection, the denizens look remarkably alike. Ranging from brown to black to platinum dyed blonde hair, from crew cuts to dreadlocks to $100 haircuts, the people of Marseille share something in common: they are incredibly fashionable and good-looking. They resemble modern takes of ancient Egyptians.

This port city is teeming with life. Though modern docks have been built north of the downtown, the old port is still stocked with hundreds of privately owned boats, and thus is picturesque year round. In the summer, fishmongers and trinket salespeople gather around the old port's terminus. The tourist bars and restaurants are filled with just that: tourists from England, Germany, America, Ireland, Scotland. They pay higher prices for inferior food and drinks, but that's o.k. because it keeps the real, locally known places less crowded. There's always crowds. From eight a.m. to three a.m. So gloriously alive. So gloriously not America.

The view from the port is formidable: Fort St. Jean on one side, Fort St. Nicolas on the other. There's the apartment building frontage that cloisters the *Panier,* one of the oldest and most wonderful districts of the city, a Protestant cathedral spiring in the distance, and the Pharo, built by Napoleon III overlooking it all. The city, unventured in, looks like an accretion of limestone populated with a million intricate fossils worth a closer look, discovery. Where to start?

NOTRE DAME

The cathedral bears the gunshot wounds left there by Germans. It is a fortified building, with ramparts and a drawbridge over where there was once a moat. Inside, piped-in voices of monks sing. The smell of candles burning. Votive paintings done by locals and treasured as secret works of art. Wooden boats hang in mobiles. The ceiling adorned in a Byzantine mosaic of angels and requisite Christian glory. In an adjoining alcove, long white candles can be bought, or stolen. But the interior of this majestic work of architecture is a frail man-made rival to the real beauty this focus point of the city dwells on.

The view from the church's hilltop position is three hundred and sixty degrees. From its terrace, the mountains that hem in the populace look like solidified waves not going anywhere. The Mediterranean stretches out into a blue of distance, towards the Orient – and cargo and ferry ships languorously cruise its sheet-metal waters.

What the cathedral's function is, and its placement serves, is obvious. What so many American cities lack is such a center point – a location from which everything can be seen. The golden virgin poised atop the dome can, in turn, be seen from anywhere below. It is a point of observation, where perspective can be achieved. And it, unlike a Sears Tower, or World Trade Center, or Sky Needle, or HOLLYWOOD sign, is not overwhelming in its significance. It merely is what it is. A centering of the immediate cosmos.

Here, fidelity to religion is nothing other than lax. In a country almost completely Catholic, only around fourteen percent of the population attends church. This is not the point. Catholicism is on a continual back burner of the mind; its traditions are not forgotten, rather melded into a way of life, and existing as such (in non-existence), so a balance is met. The famous craft of *Santons,* figurines based on a local rendition of the biblical myth, is one example.

These clay painted figurines sport the local dress and occupations of the region. A man carrying a bundle of sticks, a woman with a slaughtered rabbit, and the *ravi:* the village idiot enraptured at the birth of that famous baby. It is what differentiates France from the commercialization of religion (especially Christmas) in the U.S. Everything is done with style, a twist and blend of location and semi-logical mutation of thought.

Once, meeting with an American who has made this corner of the landscape his home for the last fifteen years, he complained of the lack of spirituality of the city. Did he know St. Victor's church contains underground crypts and dates from the fifth century? That Fort St. Jean was a Templar establishment, now containing remnants of a chapel. That there is a street celebration of the black madonna. Perhaps the community-oriented brand of religious theatricality no longer exists, but the deep, Jungian, mythical connections to religious ceremony are still vibrant, pulsating as regularly as quartz stone.

What acts as a distraction to the option of the monastic way of life is as plain as day: topless beaches, sensuous rock and sand playgrounds, U.S.-modeled fast food restaurants, the mentality of one person to a car, the filmic drivel from southern California that surmounts the kiosks (more so movie billboards in the south), the fascination of the American invention of an invented way of life.

In the *pâtisserie,* the shelves are stocked with more kinds of edible works of art than a clairvoyant could dream of: *pains au chocolat, sablés, millefeuilles, religieuses, paris-brests, jalousies, forêts-noires.* What they're pushing now is a round plop of dough with sugar on top, a hole in the middle. When asked what this too familiar thing was, the baker said, shrugging, it was a gourmet American recipe – *le donut.*

MISTRAL

The mistral is a wind. Technically speaking, it is born by the presence of a depression in the Gulf of Genoa. Cold air from the peaks of the Alps funnels into the Rhône valley; picking up speed near Valence, this mass of air becomes an entity of pure energy and blows whatever is in its way, away. Its duration lasts from one to three to six, even up to nine days.

It comes in bursts, ebbs and flows of dry air. Sometimes, it arrives as a constant force, knocking over trees, uplifting roofs, downing antennas, dispersing clothes from the laundry line, and causing havoc.

Cats commit suicide when the mistral arrives. Beach-goers mourn the loss of their new, expensive kites. It clears the skies and brightens them, and tempts the unknowing to leave the safety of their homes. It keeps hatmakers and milliners in business. It knocks on doors and windows throughout the night.

Basically, it pisses everyone off.

It has been known to reverse the direction of those on mopeds. It has raised boats from their moorings. It has tumbled fences of stone. It deposits leaves and refuse on well-kept terraces. It efficiently dries laundered bed sheets hanging outdoors, minutes before it rips them to shreds. It de-fruits trees. It disperses seeds into the sea that will eventually become buddings in foreign countries.

It inhabits your clothes, when walking in it, and tries to remove them, by force, or by its deposits of sand and sycamore seeds. It creates new hair styles. It increases gas mileage if you happen to be driving in its direction. If riding a bicycle, it blows directly into your face no matter what way you turn to avoid it.

It is the topic of small talk when it's in town.

The mistral howls and screams in celebration of itself. One suspects that fish swim deeper the days it is around. It prunes unsightly shrubbery. If it also happens to be raining, it is better to hide in a telephone booth, for days, until it has calmed. It tinges the air with a bitter pill of coldness, as sharp as an icicle.

In its ability to dismiss fog, mist, pollution, it brings the surrounding mountains closer, and gives to them the appearance that they are moving seaward. It tears clouds into wispy shreds, knots the threads, and then burns them with matches of sunlight, spears of reflection off the water.

It bankrupts outdoor markets and stalls racing horses.

The mistral is a reminder that we are merely the pawns of nature; the forces that engendered us, and human folly in general, are so much larger than can even be calculated, that it's best not to even try. Stay inside, lock the windows, close the doors and wait it out over the pleasant weather of steam rising off a hot cup of tea.

IMPRESSIONS

Des gueux disputent aux animaux les os jetés à la poubelle, des milliers d'hommes et de femmes ramassent les mégots, le chien épie l'homme, le rat épie le chat, et tous lorgent, parmi les ordures vers le même morceau de viande pourrie.

Joseph Roth
Croquis de Voyages
Paris: Editions du Seuil, 1994.

Things you don't see much in America profoundly strike your attention here. The occurrence and reoccurrence of circuses. If not broadcast on television, then live, in fairgrounds, under a real big top. At least once a month. It is always the same menu: high wire acts, women riding elephants, strong men, expert jugglers, flame/sword swallowers, maniacally acrobatic men, more clowns than are ever necessary, very skimpy costumes. Soundtracked American and British background music, sometimes with added verses in French.

Random productions of Guignol – his bright red and yellow mug on nearly every corner. Endless variations on this one particular puppet theme. Pagan religious ceremonies diluted into the kitsch of the contemporary. Homunculus with stick whose consummate act is to hit others.

Parades and public masques, with music and Halloween-like costumes. Sugar-coated apples. Traveling carnivals, the rides named in English: Dragonfly, Whirl and Twist, NASA Rocket, Speedway of Thrills. A difference in the carny culture, the people here are relatively well-dressed, lack tattoos, and are friendly and don't harass passersby into wasting their money. They are quite willing to give away their plastic, or stuffed, junk as prizes.

Telephone booths lack vandalism and graffiti. Pigeons stay up in the rooftops. Seagulls on the beach don't beg for food. Less trash on hiking trails. Restaurants empty on weeknights. Street-lights that don't blink on and off, flooding the quiet empty rues at night in pools of yellow.

Mediterranean

La mer est d'un bleu presque violet, au listel de l'horizon.
André Suarès
"Paysage Antique" de Idées et Visions

The Mediterranean is a liquid crystal desert. It represents, on good days, infinity at its calmest. Unlike the beaches of, say southern California, the intersection of sea and land here is not a huge sandy border, a margin that says: the beach. Instead, it invades the land, in bays, it laps at the earth at the delta of the Camargue, it beats a certain rhythm on the rocks above which the city resides.

On windy days, it raises a surf, one to five foot swells hardly grand enough for the desperate surfers to make any use of, but still they try. Currently, wind surfing is the rage – brightly-colored sails, like flags of yet-established countries, crisscross the water's surface in a sea parade. Sailboats are numerous, usually small versions of the larger, older types. Rarely are the mostly uninhabited islands visited. From a distance, they look desolate and inviting.

Under the water, aquatic life teems. Sea slugs, schools of fish, anemones, starfish, eels, crabs, urchins, move about completely undisturbed in the cooler months of the year. In the spring and summer, these creatures bear with the disturbances and fondlings of curious humans, and wait out infrequent storms with the patience of sirens.

Around Marseille, the hills seem to gradually rise from the basin of water, then quickly and steeply staircase. They form formidable cliffs and outcroppings in the surrounding wild areas, the *calanques,* south of the city, and serve as remote, weather eroded, in places lush, in others, barren, refuges from city life and virtual stockpiles of solitude.

There are underwater caves with famous pre-historic paintings, one featuring "penguins" and handprints. There are white stepping stone rock hills that sink into the below. There are grassy plains and plateaus that diminish abruptly in the snow of returning waves. There are rock and sand beaches that soon will be full of beautiful, tan, more than half nude sun worshippers, but are quite empty and spacious in the off-season months. An endless amount of wandering awaits those willing.

Less than an ocean and more than a great lake, the Mediterranean is just what it is. In moonlight, it offers an enchanting mirror that dares you to attain its surface. It smells of salt and iodine, is clear when viewed from up close, deeply (unrealistically) blue from afar on a sunny day. It has the ability to flux from every color within the grey, blue, green, white, spectrum. It strums its instrument constantly, putting those susceptible to sleep and looks good enough to drink.

It offers up shells, seaweed, polished stones with Zen inscriptions carved into them, driftwood, and minutely sculptured peach seeds. It replenishes the mind in its being a body of water, that perhaps, shouldn't be there. Something about it, a vastness, a lucidity, that evades even the finest tuned of senses and requires one, upon leaving it, to almost immediately, want to return.

COMMERCE

There is more stuff than anyone could ever, would ever want to buy. All things under the sun, anything that is "fashionable", arrive here and are replicated, cheaply, without threat of dearth. From every type imaginable of sunglasses, to clothes, to shoes, computers, cars, motorcycles, trinkets, books (who is translating American and British fiction so quickly?), toys, bicycles, basically your whatever you want.

In the downtown, in small stores, fabrics from the east can be bought cheaply, from Turkish rugs to African tablecloths. Secondhand traders stock the most current titles of American, Brit, East African, Algerian, Japanese, popular music (including U.S. independent labels). Junk markets are held once a week and sell everything from wallets to plants to spices to fresh fish, herbs, really the recipe for the alchemist bent on living well. Shopping, in the general, browsing sense can take up to two weeks of constant investigation into the numerous stores, and small-time vendors, department stores, sadly modern super malls, and merchandise districts. It is a consumer's dreamland that represents what the West is all about: treasures from lands near and abroad, so much useful and non-items that this business of capitalism generates in partnerships of crime. There's no hint that this money-based system is an idea that has run its course: after purchasing anything one can desire, it becomes almost a monotonous theatre of mime – exchanging shiny silver and gold coins (representing nothing) for the unneeded item of desire (formed, colored, shaped, nothing). And if the particular vendor doesn't have exactly what you seek, he or she'll know someone who does. An endless, vivid circle that represents only the idea of wholeness, large and empty in its center. Making life the same anywhere you go.

VERS TOULOUSE

It is a city that is much nearer to the West. It is a maze unto itself, full of stores and shops selling the latest clothes, music, sunglasses, gadgets. Strange how many of these newest of new items look as if they were designed in the late 1970s. But that is mere trend, as trends are excuses for what is un-needed, with the requisite undercurrent of statement.

Toulouse is surprisingly large, the country's fourth city, with a mélange of inhabitants, although this is hard to discover when in the *centre ville*. The people look oddly pale for being denizens of a southern French city; the women seem to have larger bodies, the men look more "northern", but these might be tricks of perception. Perhaps the race of Cathars, who are said to have invented the kiss as a greeting (as an exchange of breath), had truly been obliterated from the genetic pool, and the populace is now represented by the conquering Albigensians. The fantasy of speculation.

Though large, the city lacks a self-portrait. Situated on a plain in between mountain ranges, it doesn't have much of a characteristic topography, other than a bisecting, slow moving river. It is a mass of old, beautiful architecture – cathedrals, chapels, villas, monuments that rise unexpectedly out of the mishmash of well-cared for ancient lodgings, and of course, the eyesores of modernity.

The eeriness that it evokes is most felt when one is within its interior. There is no view. There is no off-in-the-distance. There is nothing to gauge a pedestrian's smallness, or relationship to the larger world, other than the reflections of its grand architecture in the most immediate shop window.

Perhaps this larger view is unnecessary. There are many bookstores that have extensive libraries about the Languedoc-Roussillon area, hundreds of tomes on the city's architecture, history, and lore (it seems the extinct Cathars are a goldmine in this respect), books in English, German, Spanish, and Italian, a slew of World Art stores, and more restaurants in which a human could possibly eat given the brevity of life. Toulousians need not venture outside their city's boundaries to get a taste, feeling, sensation of the riches of earthly life.

LES PONTS DE TOULOUSE

The smaller, less used, older ones are the most beautiful. Pont Neuf is the most famous. They connect the two halves of the city like vertebrae. What lies beneath them is more interesting, for the bridges provide the architecture of an underworld.

Along the quays of Toulouse people satiate their desire for the sea, an open space. Students, a large amount of the populace (at least a quarter and a *quartier*), lounge in the sun, read, juggle and re-enact other medieval pastimes. They smoke, drink, talk of love, life, and sex, read newspapers, and creatively exist.

It is along the river where one can find Moroccans eager to sell their contraband of hashish sticks. They call out to passers-by "cigarette" simply to purchase attention. When responded to, they let you know that they have hashish, powerful stuff too, home-made. Though you have passed a street musician sporting a Visa-Mastercard sign, the spicemen take only hard currency.

They'll ask where you're from and tell you about their lives back home, across the sea. They won't cut you the best of deals but they'll share a few moments asking about the greener pastures from where you come. They'll give you a cheeky, stained-teeth smile, shake your hand and tell you to come back when you have enough pocket money you don't care about. *Salut, mes amis.*

ASIDE: Coastal memorieS

And so it is almost a desert. With a cold wind, freezing even pools of sand in the hills. Puddles of salt turning into balls of crystals, rock near ocean. Pebbles washed up – finely crafted layers, a beach of worrying beads. Like a hand-rolled cigarette, only tasting better, not the metallic rasp in the throat. Hair and veils receding. Needing to wash.

Washing.

It blows and it blows and it blows. It blows through you. It penetrates bone. It is as bitter as smoke. It dries the laundry quick. It burns holes of salt into your clothes. As the woman in the world of her, your life, that one desired, just look – every movie – the one that gets away. One you cannot have.

Around her, and her city, there are hills painted Turkish, that is blue and light green, always black always white. Outlines of jagged obelisk tipped topography, a calcite horizon layered in brush stroke green, mint needles of dry pine.

Wind from the north, worse than light.

CRUSADES,
SPOILS OF VICTORY

Because the hostilities in the former Soviet bloc countries serve as a modern little crusade and whet the European, or Western (two terms yet to be defined) appetite for a theater of war spectacle, habits die hard. We bomb Babylonia sucking the fruits of its gardens, the taming of the Bower, our bad habits never stop dying.

Being greatly disliked on the basis of foreign-ness, a chin or a nose cast in a certain way, helps to hurry exodus. A wonderful historical period, mind you, but the time's right up to it, one long wait in the anteroom of the mechanic. Chicks in swimsuits on the wall calendars.

The beach remains undivided, for the most, adult parts. The etymology of adultery made apparent. A mathematical equation for the numerical relation to the amount of articles of clothing not there. Yet, there.

Mediterranean full of beautiful, easily the world's most beautiful women, and men, bathing, together. The men selling boards of junk, some indeed needed, multiwonderful colors, sunglasses, bracelets, friendship bands, these flags. Then the same men out of their skull yellow red black caps in the lousy bars filled with but older, tiring men, smoke and smell of old dreams predictably quixotic, in half reality, it all going out with its 2 a.m. lights, dingy fluorescent. They go home yelling, singing, pissing where the dogs earlier did, kicking the trash in the sewers like bills of their own spilt paychecks.

LANDSCAPE,
WITH WHITE DESERTS

Between the metropolis of Marseille and the resort town of Cassis, paradise is found. A stretch of mountains, or hills that have characteristics of alpine regions, plateaus barren of trees but lush in short, ground-clinging brush and flowering plant life, canyons that appear out of the illusion of flatland that contain hidden niches of pine trees and level areas perfect for nomadic habitation. A jagged skyline crumbles in steep drop offs into the sea, within the precipices and fortifications of bone white calcium are inlets of the sea – clear blue water, sand and rock beaches, stone platforms that lead one to the realms of Atlantis, and beyond.

It is a landscape that must be experienced, for pictures/representations of it convey a meager meaning of what being within its confines and among its liberating distances *doesn't* attempt to signify. In the short view, this land's counterpart, or sister region, is the American West. The geographical, minus the Mediterranean, similarities are striking.

Inscribed within its winding, maniacally carved topography are neolithic caves. A most recent, and ancient, example, is the *Grotte Cosquer,* discovered in 1991, an addition to the amazement found in the caves of Lascaux. Caves dot any detailed map of the area, and unlike the rigid control schemes of the park systems in America, these places can be visited and explored freely, that is, if you can get to them. Perched on cliff sides, or near summits, they provide a destination for a rigorous outing, especially in the months of summer. Inside their dark chambers is a mysterious humidity, one that smells of the past, and promises a dose of fear, anxiety, and discovery. They respire with a sound of deep silence and dripping water. Plants with blackened roots adorn the walls. Crystals, like immediate stars, twinkle in crevasses in their mineral skies. The remaining unpilfered stalactites and mites are as formidable as Roman column-work and shapeshift into golems, sphinxes, and griffins under the transmogrifying power of a flashlight. Perhaps their potential of being pilgrimage places for followers of New Age religions will not be realized in the near future, but their semblances to centers of vortices are undeniable. There is a secret power contained within these cavities, a return to the womb, a space for centering the consciousness within the earth. And the caves are open, in all seasons, for the amount of eternity that the curious are willing to spend in them.

It is a preserved, unspoiled region. Fires have decimated much of the forest, though large expanses, and strips of oases, invite expedition. The coastline has no parallel. Blocks of calcium so rugged, pointed, occasionally flattened into small plateaus, and naturally breaking into *calanques* (isolated bays), in which a private beach or bathing pool is impossible not to find. In the crowded months of the summer, hikers and fishermen pass by on the balconies of trails hundreds of feet above the sea, and nude bathers act as sentinels guarding nothing on outcrops within the sea; for the most part, the only visible inhabitants are gulls who cry like babies to let you know they are there. And watching.

It is doubtful that this area can be described competently in words, and even less so in a medium such as photography or painting. Its essence is irresistible yet resists any kind of human captivation. The effort is worth the challenge. One charming aspect is that the southern reaches of Marseille, although sparsely populated with restaurants and beach residences, are not over-developed. The Marseillais respect this wilderness for what it is: a wild moonscaped land left to the devices of erosion, regeneration, the pure abstraction of stone, a paysage of little thought and complete being. And then there is the world below.

LEAGUES

Looking up from the depth of ten feet below the sea, the waves breaking into surf on rock, presents another weather. The surface of the water resembles clouds erupting with rain or snow, the cliffs are covered in sea vegetation, with creatures such as urchins and mussels, and look like the sides of not so arid steppe. Fish, swimming singly or in bands of many, like air or spacecraft working through docking maneuvers. Otherworldly is the feeling, yet its deterioration into cliché gives a clue to a truer nature.

This is the first world, a primeval one that is immediately recognized. The quietude under water is eerie. The lack of horizon and surrounding blueness obliterate a sense of perspective: all that can be sensed is within feet from the viewer. It leads one to think if fish have a concept of the future, or even distance in a greater meaning than what is continuously arriving within the range of sight. There is no meaning in this realm, other than the bizarre phenomenon we label life. The maritime world is clearly existential.

Breaking the threshold of surface, where distance reigns, are arid islands, white, barren, torturous in contour, ironic reminders of the inherent contrast and the paradox of being. Thorns of desert relentlessly weathering amidst plains of life bearing water.

Easy access clarity. On the crowded summer beaches, approximately five to ten percent of sunbathers even enter the sea. The secrets of the underworld can be revealed for the minimum price of a pair of goggles or a diving mask. It seems the topographies of almost nude human bodies hold more interest than the kingdom of Poseidon, constantly churning in life, just below a blue extending horizon.

MATTERS OF A MORE EARTHLY DEVICE

There is, as we all know, the French kiss. Especially famous among grade- and high-schoolers, it is an initiation into the seductive powers of the culture(?), language(?), passion of the stereotypical Latin populace. More interesting, although not as pleasing, is the French greeting.

We all know what it is, but for those who are in need of briefing, this gesture/movement/ritual is extended to friends and family, never strangers (unfortunately, thus making get-togethers among friends more fun). It might be described as a near hug, with the placement of each cheek next to those of the one being greeted (cheek to cheek), touching or near touching, with the addition of actual kisses (what we call "pecks" in American) to the aforementioned cheeks, or most often, in the air slightly above and in the direction of the cheeks of the one being greeted. In some regions, this process is repeated, making it four kisses in two complex, bird-like, mock-courting ritualistic movements. In other regions, it is done only once, and in some rare cases, an odd thrice.

Let it be said that it is an interesting, intimate, wonderful way of bonding. Especially when the one to be greeted is an attractive member of the opposite sex. A nose full of his or her hair, cologne or perfume, and the proximity to his or her ear and nape enhances any social situation. The problem that arises with those of non-Franco cultures, for instance Anglo-American, is that one is never sure when exactly to extend this type of greeting, since it can be extended to children up to the age of 20 (young men included and depending on the personality) and older women, depending upon geniality.

The greeting has eroded into a somewhat forced practice, thus, and this is only supposition, the kiss-in-air mutation, with theatrically practiced and pronounced kiss sounds and puckering. If we dare delve into the meaning of the practice, so late into the twenty-first century, it seems to announce that there are close bonds that link family and friends, beyond superstitions that build walls and carve out personal spaces, without the need for extensive elbow room. Yet today it is becoming a ritual of days gone by; a practice as heartfelt as children in catechism crossing themselves; a routine disconnected from its sense of meaning. Un-revitalized, the curse of all tradition.

LES FANTÔMES

Strangely enough, there is a decidedly bizarre lack of the belief in the true-to-life manifestation of ghosts in the south of France, though there is the daily adherence to rituals of the quasi-supernatural. The bread ceremony, including the sacrificial eating of its tip, *le quignon,* a pyramid point of the crust, what many think to be the most delicious morsel. It's best eaten immediately. As in walking out the door of the bakery, excusing yourself from in between the musty scarves of old ladies, towards more vital places: bus stops or metro gates, escalators descending into a steaming underground. Into the smell of rain or what pigeons leave on sidewalks, streets.

Candles are lit in the midst of bad storms. Saints have visited the region and have even inhabited local caves. In the cathedral near the coast and in the extreme southern part of the city (closer to Italy), there is an aquarium of blessed fish, thus assuring a bountiful catch for the fishermen of the quarter.

Downtown on a crowded day of Saturday shopping, socializing, in general being-aliveness, it is strange to find most of the small "chichkebabaries" not full of people. The only times they aren't: Ramadan. Surprising to see the number of its adherents by not seeing them.

Money (gold and silver colored coinage) or even teeth containing those precious metals, are sealed into a wall of the house. This tradition is kept, be it rarely, to keep the treasure safe and to create an aura of fortune, good luck, the power of materiality blessing those tenants who believe in its antiquated cult.

Superstition is not overtly upheld, or at least admitted, by the French. They seem a generally skeptic lot. Especially when asked if they believe in ghosts. *Perhaps,* they say, *living in castles.* They themselves haven't seen them, or experienced them, or even have gone looking for them in cemeteries at night, preferably in winter. Their resting places are behind walls and locked at night. Spectral little kingdoms unto nowhere.

If you break a clear glass accidentally, it's good luck. Probably invented by café owners serving *pressions* in factory-given glassware. *Mère nécessité.*

A baguette of bread placed upside-down on a table is a very bad sign. It stems from the history that the executioner, the one who supervised the running of the guillotine, would receive his bread in such a way. People still avoid a casual placement of the daily grain. It is also believed that prostitutes were given bread in this manner to symbolize their assumed work stance. Either way, it's still a mild shocker.

Friday the 13th is regarded as a lucky day, and not one to dread in fear of a homicidal maniac skinning one alive. Though full moonlight is known to be able to change the color of clothes, obviously the moon as a super huge mirror can be justified scientifically, thus believed in. In some circles, it is said to have the ability to alter the pigments of watercolor or oil paintings. This yet remains to be seen by one skeptic.

Because the green dye used in theatre vestments was dyed with arsenic, this hue for clothing is rarely seen on television or even the stage. And carnations are given as a mild reprimand, or critique. These are all things everybody knows.

When you give someone a knife they give you a coin. Same with a handkerchief.

A hat on the bed is an omen of death.

A spider at night brings hope, a morning spider, mourning.

The monotonous pageantry of strikes

November, December, January, February is strike season. In differing years, different cities, or regions. It's usually desperately needed services such as the mail (almost a crime), buses/metros, trucks that deliver gas, France Telecom — oh, just about anything that one would never dream about doing without in the States. It's a bargaining tool forged in the old days that still possesses its well-proven power to twist the arms of others. Why the government, or management, just can't say Uncle is anyone's guess.

As these words are being written, it's the buses, and sort of, the post office. That is, in the case of the latter, some mail, of national origin, is being delivered. International mail is still coming through, but at a reduced level. How much of it I miss, or gets lost, displaced, shredded, burnt to crispy cinders, is an unknown {the empty set}.

Demonstrations occur in a place in front of the Prefecture (seat of the Departement). Sometimes they are spirited and include amplified music, dancing, effigies, banners, in one case gorilla costumes. People gathering, of course marching and singing, in Marseille, little to never any skirmishes or anything approaching violence. Spirited discussions fit the bill.

Years ago, in Montpellier, students actually got riled up enough to break windows, collect beautiful wooden café chairs (crafted in Spain) and build them into great flaming bonfires that worked well as blockades, until they were reduced into a smoldering mess.

What does one do when these strikes and processions do disrupt the normal nine to five day (well, 9-12/2-7)? The solution is: use it as an excuse to not go to work, and if the weather is permitting, enjoy the outdoors. Yes, debts pile up, more confusion will arrive in the form of missed payments, delayed deliveries, shortened office hours, but then there's the beach, the hills, and sea to attend to.

LES GOUDES

It sounds too close to "the goods" to not be true. This tiny village at the southern extension of Marseille, and at the beginning of the wild region known as the Calanques, doesn't even try, couldn't even try, to conceal its embodiment of heaven on earth. Minutes more to the south, in what amounts to a dead end to sea, hillside, cliff, and pine forest nature (with looming monuments for emphasis), only the tinier inhabitation of Callelongue rivals its outcrop and watery edge-of-nothingness.

This is where paradox collides / where desert meets sea / forested cliffs overlook a forest of life and plants on the shelves in the Mediterranean / carpets of resilient shore vegetation manage to survive and bloom / the views are of continents, of endless Dovers, falling into an abyss of ocean (isn't it really) / wind is the only song with crooning of seagulls / the western world in the style of a true-to-life Japanese print / the manifest symbol of both beginning and end materialized (preter)naturally / a place beyond pictures or words.

OF VIEWS AND SMOKE

*29 Septembre [1928] Samedi. Marseille — A 7 heures du
soir ai pris du haschish après avoir longuement hésité.
...*

*j'étais effectivement allongé sur le lit avec la certitude
absolue de ne pouvoir être dérangé dans cette ville de
plusieurs centaines de milliers de personnes où un seul
homme me connaît . . .*

> Walter Benjamin
> *Sur le haschich et autres écrits sur la drogue*
> trans. by Jean-François Poirier
> Collection "détroits". Paris: Christian
> Bourgois, 1993.

It is a city without beginning — middle — end, endless veins of
circulation and cells of vibrant, chaotic life. Which doesn't mean
it's not sixty percent dead. It is as dead as the Greek renegade
pioneer hippies buried with their cutlery in mounds above the
port. It's as dead as the Roman legions who marched and built its
streets (for marching) and ate here inventing restaurants, drank
here and gambled for clothes and women, who fucked here slept
here shat here vomited here and cried here and maybe sent
thoughts from here if not some kind of ancient postcards by
taking a rock and saving it for a lover. Anyway, anyhow the
memories are so vivid as to lead the mind and spirit back to its

days which are now with eternity making it so in an invisible chemistry, pure alchemical chemistry of sun (first), sea, sea air, salt, clarity (becoming rarer, but yet), and the idea if not the geophysical Morse alphabetics of islands.

There for you to have it, being anything from the best in life (free to not so expensive) to the worst (very expensive to free) and wrapped in the most beautiful packaging that natural selection ironically randomly (the beauty of it) provides. Okay not so much so with pastries in their Christmas boxes replete with ribbons and bows to sandwiches – chichkebabs or merguez or if you're homesick, *tournedos frites* bound like sacrificial fish in Japanese paper with a cheap imitation of it (Amurican napkin) to men in fine suits in fine Italian-made cars, the suits too, the men too, to women in their Sunday best EVERY DAY and boats from kayak to galleon to yacht that are the disgusting Cadillacs of water, flowing here and there just as smooth as money. You learn things about the sea when it's deep deep blue it is cold and green it is like a bath and how we should exist surrounded by and in a thin mist of water – our life element what we mostly are anyway. Waves that break in each other's general direction and shine and shimmer like immediate stars and yet stars we can't touch, only experience in our minds not as bright points of light or supernovas or all-engulfing black holes of a rudimentary evilness but the stuff we are made of and hence completely abstract portraits of ourselves and all the people (otherselves) that have existed in the world. We name them and draw pictures with them and travel under their kind guidance and study them to try to reach them even though distances of such greatness are not relative and in their not being so ARE and we travel into the slosh of space not knowing it is just this blackness that keeps the

71

whole ball running, the big blue and green, listlessly spinning without meaning without place name without metaphors. Here and now.

Movement always of small boats, tourist barges, traffic and pedestrians sometimes local, sometimes lost in the port. Where there's water intersecting with city, water non-Venetian though smelling of it, pond, it attracts a most interesting rat life. Elegant diners engaged in assignations during three-hour meals including well-oiled cigarette cases, small tips, foot play under the table and plans for an eveningtude that creates seaside windows to unfog. Bums watch and don't write anything down, if only to memory or recognition that's so cheap and easy it comes in the blink of an eye. Elle est bonne. Even the workers make it a parade with their 5 o'clock loaves of bread or pizzas recently taken from woodfire ovens in boxes in front of their work-weary chests that have filtered two too many cigarettes and cups of steaming coffee in pursuit of the yes tired and bedraggled ever-resuscitated American Dream.

Poppies are growing everywhere and as instantly they begin to wrinkle and fold themselves up into cylinders of blood, scroll droplets, faraway tears of the sun. Old woman with a mole growing on her nose as another nose, but a dog's nose, lives in an abandoned World War Two bunker and even she has everything that she needs other than the always present nothing that so icily remembers itself as a reflection remembered in a mirror so made manifest in the empty seats on the bus making its rounds, dumbly through the city and at traffic lights pausing to let out a sigh of steam or is it an exhalation that boredom mother of necessity brings. The things that we know we will never know. Apparent as air it is in a foreign country (but not too far because it's impossible to get away) where everything is different therefore by definition the same but only in a new way. The observer is observed in you, too.

Hedonism in action, full swing, whenever the sun's out (mostly) and in force under its own flag: a light blue cross on a white background. It is spring and people are re-entering the world. Beaches, coastal parks, city parks, the hills and mountains, everywhere that is not downtown, although *centre ville* remains crowded. The few and many who venture to the outer regions, to non-human nature, are of a certain open places mindset (agreeable). Even if it's just on the weekend and they dress in heels and dress shoes and it's a walk out on the rocks of the jetty with some bread, cheese, wine bought for pennies.

As venturesome Greeks, we are all here in the one great colony of an empire that no longer matters. We are of every race and nation, some that once warred against another to no avail but boring odyssical stories (the lesson learned) misremembered around drunken campfires. Nobody cares anymore about the conflicts, we want to talk about the quotidian: weather, travel, absinthe, the densities of differing wines, cheese skins. Scuba divers return standing placid on calm boats and easy seas hungry to see buildings attached to these green falling cliffs.

VENDAGES

Is it not a romantic thought? To pick up and leave one day. Leave the job, the somewhat predetermined existence, perhaps the wife and kids, to go to a place like the French countryside where life will daily present itself as an impressionist painting, the food will be so delicious, the air crisp and the skies luminous, and all one must do for sustenance is simply pick grapes. Work in the fields. A modern peasant life. Working in such a picturesque, fantastical environment can't be real work anyhow.

The first week of September the inland country (but from its mountains one can sense the sea) of vinefield and looping farmland around the long green creased Luberon feels like a Sahara. There are no clouds of any importance. A haze of heat and humidity lingers. By 10 a.m. it is near 90 degrees. The sky is so clear that when taken in full view, one etched and tree enshrouded hilltop to the same and yet marginally different combination of the next, it doesn't make anything but perfect sense. Flies are buzzing in swarms about eight feet high in the air preparing for the afternoon feast of animal and human. Days are brilliant, lasting for more day than is needed, or usual, or expected. One factor often not mentioned. It is unbearably hot.

Due to the expressive and unbound nature of the southern French, especially of French women donning housedresses and plastic shoe thongs, the phrase *il fait chaud* is repeated incessantly as mantra. A continual weather report of the obvious. The heat somehow provides itself a running commentary.

Weeks before this monster of a summer day (September is synonymous with fall in a northerner's vocabulary), I had volunteered my services to a family-owned wine producing affair. A business it was yet not and probably never to be. I should have read something looming into their quizzical yet polite acceptance of my skilless raw strength and pure stupidity. I thought that such a small parcel of land needed only some love and care to produce a subtle yet better by any means than Californian, Italian, Australian, stock of wine.

Let me here stress the importance of care taking in general. Of one's hair, car, wardrobe, etcetera. What I had unknowingly stumbled into was the direst of all vinicultural situations: roughly two and one half acres of *vignes sauvages*.

The vines, in the wild state as they were (and probably will remain), had not been groomed for two growing seasons. In fact, last year's crop was left to rot on the stalk to be occasionally nibbled on by passing magpies and ravens and greedily consumed by the Beaucerons, Grognon and Elsa, when they became that thirsty.

Any grapevine is a formidable entity. It is much like a skinny octopus with thorn-filled tentacles, great glowing testicular bulbs of fruit, thick meaty green leaves (and the *dolmates* they could make!), and a perfect biosphere for hungry flies. Grapevines grow in a dusty almost chalk-like soil. When one attempts to walk through a field of this earth, carrying two ten-gallon buckets full of juice-filled grapes, the feet sink into ground emitting puffs of heat-dried dust and a certain wavering of the legs.

The first step of the process is to cut the wild-growing extensions of reaching vines, but not too close to the grapes or the fruit of next season will be affected. Then, it's to tear their prickly severed limbs from the clump of vegetal mess (how the calluses bloom and burst!), then cut the grapes from the stalk, throw the firm gelatinous handful into the ever-present buckets that surround, then hoist those weights down the field lane into a truck bed that is well above shoulder height. Then return to those solemn rows of miniature trees that are about as tall as a human and continue the fête.

Not the heat nor the monotony that can be broken by eating a luscious grape, a slight buzz provided by its juice, the sun, the body filtering grape juice, not the lack of conversation due to an unending workload, it is the flies that make the chore hell on earth.

The invisible flesh-eating flies curse all effort. They force workers to wear pants and long sleeves and socks. Any body part that is left uncovered is appetizers for the beasts (literally, *les bêtes*). One's unprotected arms and legs begin to resemble those of a serious unskilled junkie. Swollen red bloody chunks, like mosquito bites surgically removed, quickly form into scabs. These scabs immediately begin to itch.

The workday begins at seven, stops for lunch sometime soon after noon, reluctantly resumes around two (when it shouldn't), and continues until dusk, which graciously appears at around seven/seven thirty. Lunch is godsend. Lunch is momentary freedom. Lunch is the evil mirror reflection of life outside of the fields. Cold clean water to remove skins of dust. The absence of the taste of one's spit. Yet every moment of not working is tinged with the yoke of the immediate future: the return to the vegetal battlefield.

Lunch, which by necessity, must be light, consists of sandwiches of cheese (you pick from the four hundred or so) and *jambon cru,* a salad with tomatoes and hot peppers and endive leaves, perhaps if lucky a grilled lamb chop, then yogurt in tiny packaged packages (sugar must be added for a boost), then coffee to revitalize. The French don't drink lunchtime coffee for the kick. It's merely for the taste. Fruit is optional and on a day like this is jokingly offered as a bowl of *raisins.* Mmmm, grapes.

It's back to the fields after doing whichever ritual one thinks will help facilitate the undeniable cliché of "backbreaking work". This toil is possible only by thoughts of dinner, the solitude of sleep and/or sex (if energy for the latter can be mustered), and the incredible view and its promise of escape to the barren pyramid of Mt. Ventoux.

A COURT OF WALLS

Throughout the Mediterranean the concept of a yard happily does not exist. Parks have wide and long expanses of manicured lawns, true, but the people, even the rich, have cultivated something better.

It's the small, compact nature of Europe that has logically led her to separate her frugal governed spaces by labyrinths of walls. In the nicer villas and private homes and in older, well-maintained apartment structures, enclosed courtyards provide inhabitants with the privacy of nature contained all for one's self, rooms forested with plant life, a synthesis of the manmade inviting in the naturally occurring.

And isn't it so much more human to construct living places that do not conform to one another, no floor plan exactly reproduced, with loose interpretations of Italianate architectural styles? With these creations existing behind stucco walls, if not ages-old stone, with the extensions of living quarters themselves opening onto the courtyards, the ground is either white gravel or as wild as a meadow.

Historic apartment buildings impress one with their bulk and matching orange tile roofs, but it is the houses that grow geometrically outward like mineral formations characterizing the biomorphic quality of the region. There are châteaux and monumental houses built to resemble them. There are ugly modern buildings that, in my opinion, Corbusier's Marseille apartment complex illustrates in multicolor. Touted as a site of some repute and notice in guidebooks, I had passed it for months on a bus route until finally I overheard some passengers pointing it out on a dreary rainy day commute. There was nothing else to inspire talk that day.

But the houses, the simple villas one hundred years old or more (and some younger) are examples of how what was created once is continually salvaged, improved, added onto – a grafting of respect and practicality. The effect is one of cubistic, mismatched birdhouses of differing shapes and levels. From the outside, these highly livable places resemble the interior of such American follies as the Winchester mansion.

Shutters are painted resplendent or are equally beautifully shedding skins of old paint. How the roof tiles seem to undulate under the sun. How glimpses gleaned from a resident's entering and opening of a gate allow a passerby to briefly feel invited to the mystery of their singular courtyard that is constantly vesseling daylight and gesturing its green limbs "welcome". Piranesi for the first time in his life entering a zoo.

More surprising and amazing is the secret that these houses, villas, and millions of apartments contain inside. There is a secret place. The altar of life. Where the human container opens up on itself: the terrace.

There is no American comparison to the terrace. It is not a deck. It is definitely not a porch. It is an open-roofed enclosure, the floor made of tile, surrounded by five to six foot walls which often include plant beds, an area to grill, an omnipresent expansive table, morning fog, blankets of brightness, cotton candy sunsets, and stars overhead.

The terrace is like having one's own private picnic ground. A place to sunbathe (preferably nude). A link to the outdoors that is always a step away. The terrace is where one reads a book while warming the body on the sun-baked tiles or a place to smoke and contemplate views of distant hills, clouds, sea, or other rooftops hiding terraces. A terrace is an invitation to exercise or lounge. To reinvigorate the body or continue the night's slow progression of dreamtime.

In the premier étage apartment in which I stayed, not only was there a large terrace (the largest of all physical spaces) opening on a southwest view of the city, above it was another small terrace where pigeons once rooked. From this higher level, the entire expanse of the city not absconded by populated hillsides could be seen, the white and green banded crescent of enclosing topography, the Mediterranean sea and its weather, views into most of the blocks' courtyards and apartment windows (although I never really looked). A most secluded enclave that allows one the cosmopolitan appreciation of what it is like to be a bird in a city.

Much of daily life, except during the blustery cold rain winter months, is carried out on the terrace. Hung laundry, most meals, or warm night slumber, and the best activity of all: watching the street below.

The streets in France contain life at most hours of the day and night. The country is so vibrant, unabashed, active, alive. The streets provide a carnival of vibrancy with songs of traffic skirmishes, advice-giving from and to those who hardly know each other, spontaneous bursts of remembered melodies, the name of a friend yelled after one too many pre-dinner pastises, a sometimes parade of children celebrating a day sponsored by the city: adults and kids dressed as fruit. There is only one response to all of this. Why not!

There is also usually an ever-present din: jackhammers at 7:30 a.m. for street improvements or to lay the new invention of cable lines, heated discussions after strolling back from the park over a lost game of pétanque, obsessive bakery runs for the third fresh baguette of the day which involves stopping the car in the midst of rush hour traffic and the line behind that one person eagerly becoming vocal.

At anytime of the day there are women looking lovely, men hurrying and smoking and no one, no one ever looking up.

The terrace inspired my creation of a zen garden in miniature (as one should be). In one of the dormant flowerbeds, a chunk of cemented-together quarried stone, I planted vegetation native to the *collines*. Wild asparagus, strands of thyme and rosemary, tufts of moss. With sand and shells and rocks and driftwood and sea salt-eroded unknowables found on the beach. With these elements, I began to compose. Added to the mix were religious medals found in a tin box under the stairs, tarnished in forgottenness – luminescent blue Virgin medallions, blood-rusted Christs on crosses. Old jewelry casing and sea shell buttons. Half buried in sand and fine beach pebbles and branches of *immortelles*, they provided landmarks, artifacts for the eye to puzzle over. Then release.

TWO SIDES OF
THE SAME COIN

Tuscany or Provence. Provence or Tuscany. With Americans, it's a battle between the two. Who will win our much unneeded crown of the most beautiful, the best place to be, or the best place to want to live (if we had sufficient culture to do so). Or is it those two regions that possess what our Malibus, our Martha's Vineyards, our Montereys, our coming close to Europe but not nearly it San Francisco can never possess. History. A psychological connection to the Old World. Africa, Asia as lost siblings.

If the question vexes, the choice is simple to make. Find all the tourist books, coffee table tomes (there are more than ever needed, yet not enough to capture the essences) and in a completely arbitrary manner, compare the elements: ridgelines in view of villas and the other way around, the flora, fauna, foliage, qualities of light, textures of landform, weave of blankets of fields and, though imponderably unfair – judge them. Play Solomon and judge.

It might be in the way photographers desire to mime the somber effects of Renaissance painters that Tuscany is portrayed in such tones. Darkly majestic. It also might be in the secret whim to be an amateur Van Gogh that Provence is nearly always portrayed in guidebook ecstasy: unreal colors in blinding sunshine. A composition of treed hillsides village stone and fenced by local rocks. All painstakingly arranged to pay homage to the schools of painting that invented these topographies.

Provençals could not, would not even consider comparing their lands to another's, and if asked to consider the Italian countryside, they would characterize it as a completely different place, a viable vacation retreat. It is strange and mundane that these two places have won so much admiration in America. Both are unyieldingly complex, remarkable in history and possessing a perfection so fine that paintings or photographs can hardly represent.

As the dream of the American West was filmed in such diverse places as southern Utah, northern Arizona, and the Mojave, these places promised Europeans a mythological sacred locus where the stories of the past, histories, could merge in a clear desert aridity of ahistory. In the American deserts, visions could be reinterpreted, redone with modern relevance. On the flipside, Tuscany and Provence play the obverse role in the American phenomenon.

These are regions that supply myths for moviemakers and dreamers on a smaller scale. The birthplaces of the eternal return. In Italy and France, these are the regions where everything is good and pure and mystical and linked to a past that America cannot ever reproduce and must regularly celebrate from the safety of great distance both physical and mental.

La villE

Take the day to do absolutely nothing; there's nothing to do anyway. Pleasure outweighs work in this glorious, burnt white rock and Aleppo-pined cityscape, sun bleeding orange roofs spilling in to the nothingness, mirror of the sea. Days are devised to purely experience the day: smell of fresh baguettes cooking and infinite other delicious pastries, coated in glazes of real honey, filled with almonds and almond filling. Fruits shining themselves in the constant, reliable sunlight, lounging in their wooden boxes on the sidewalk, shipped from Tunisia, Morocco, bright stickers saying so on the sides.

Walk, stroll, or ride the bus, the metro: both come every seven minutes or so, never an inconvenience to be released from the burden of a car (a concept heretical in the U.S.). Marseille's only drawback, really a real inconsistency, is that the subways do stop running at nine p.m., unless there's an OM soccer match. Waiting for the bus or metro these are some of the types to be encountered: interested in you Africans who speak a broken French much better than yours will ever be seemingly always asking others for the time, North African men or women returning your stare as you both exchange this unspoken thought (*exotique!*), a congenial Marseillais who is more than willing to offer up his views on anything under that brilliant, all-illuminating Mediterranean sun – food, the weather, the current state of politics, the very nature of the sexes, the immediate future and leaning of the world in general, and, of course, architecture, fine arts, civil engineering, and the manifold and resplendent forms of desire.

Even the ride is a most pleasant experience. Passing through Greek and Roman architecture, modern businesses, above and below hills, tunnels and city centres all that animate with well-dressed people. If luck is in the air, the bus will take a side trip down the Corniche, past the long stretch of man-made beaches (*au naturel,* the coast is a rocky, violent one), and the bus will stop just past the sculpture of David, who sometimes sports briefs or other drunkenly inspired summer wear, and the beaches full with youth gloriously unarrayed. Not in the vulgarity of thongs, not unclad as they were just on the shores, but loosely dressed and smelling of sea salt, soap, body oils, and the possibility of love.

Bus rides are opportunities to view not only in a dramatic manner the shifting, stratified cityscape, but its denizens too as all classes and ages take advantage of its services. Opportunities to fall in love with the savage landscape, to see deep into the sea, to mingle with those of many nationalities and races that defy, and care little for, definition, with the goal, the single goal, of the people, the driver, the town, which is finally to enjoy to its fullest, culminating in beach, exquisite food, wine, cosmopolitan glee, money, fun, uninhibited sex, life.

Marseille noiR

In neon and halogen light (all the streetlights are purposefully yellowed) and promises of bright tomorrow sunlight, night descends. This time is bad for women – they are harassed (think of the multitude of "Mediterranean types"). For men, it's the nocturnal quotidian without as much traffic and noise and much better views of where they aren't. Fewer people. Broad streets. Fresh cool air. The promise of money making's frenzied day gone by, now it's time to spend it, even if it's not there to spend. The placidity of the port still with ships just barely bouncing in tidal flux. Emptied streets, except for the make-up plastered sad whores who were once truly beautiful, streetlights beckoning one to the next, assemblage of bars and restaurants, a *glacier* still open. Europe's calm, openness of nighttime which is definitely not rushing home to the kids of America, to crack deals gone smooth, things to do rather than sequester oneself in family and home.

Marseille's reputation makes one initially stop, pause, and think at night. Really, the crime here is local, rather than mythically international, and rarely grazes the passerby. Hold the head up straight, walk with confidence, and no one will dare to bother you. They will notice you. To be noticed is to be something. This place, thankfully, ain't America.

As a fact of matter, Marseille at night is most romantic and inspiring. At any time of the day, a pizza and two bottles of wine can be enjoyed on any of its numerous and continuous beaches, without official hassle. The laws aren't the same. There is no law against pleasure in France. Other than the proximity of yet another young couple who decide to do the same very close to your spot of infinity as they do so, deciding to remove articles of clothing in an impromptu skinny-dip.

Prurient Americans always ask, do people do it there on the beaches? Hardly, as the French have an innate quality: class. Foreplay might be begun, if even rarely, for the beaches are intimate meeting grounds where one can shed one's western garbs and be oneself for a few hours of liquid oneness that can lead anywhere: to an over-priced beachside restaurant, to an apartment somewhere just west of downtown, to a drive to Cassis, a cruise to Tunisia, really anywhere.

A few immediate eating spots: L'Américano featuring fine merguez, steak-hachés, pizza, even ice cream. Chez Paul's in the anse of les Goudes: cheap carafes of good wine, the finest view of the city outside of the city and the best pizzas; Chez Fonfon with one of the best bouillabaisses known to the area with its wonderful central location, hidden in its own calanque; the others of other places and others even waiting to be discovered. The city is open until the wee hours.

MAZARGUES

A district. A neighborhood. A place. A certain intersection of streets. An architectural relic left standing like a lonely buttress or a stranded support of an old bridge surrounded by the river it once straddled. An island for lost pigeons.

There are these blocks strung together south and west of the city, yet within the city, that once and still attempt to make up a locality, a livable entity. It was a garment and fashion district. How befitting that it should be left behind like last year's dresses. The secret way to enter the area, to enter its maze, is on foot, south and directly underneath its hidden spire of a bridge no longer walked. Of course, nobody walks the district anymore, except loyal mothers who continue to shop each day for the essentials that they trail behind them in a wheeled cart of wire. Nobody walks to it anymore due to the new widened boulevards and decent bus service. As a foreigner with no illusions or desires of ever owning a vehicle in this strange land and the liberation this implies, I still pine for those days I didn't have to drive. Points on a map attained by metro, bus, and a good deal of footwork. The only way to discover a country.

After sauntering down streets and alleys as one will do, being young and alive in Europe, counting how many *coquelicots* are blooming in between the adobe-like concrete walls and bright green-painted wooden doors, vines creeping up where invisible moisture sweats, with wildly yellow blooming supernovae of mimosa swinging overhead making the pedestrian sick for the scent of a woman's neck in the evening, a garden path leads behind modern, ugly, but livable apartment buildings. Past fields locked in chainlink limbo, as prayers are said, candles lit so those places will never become yet another modern living spread, a collection of villas as they choose to paint them now. At the school of botany, we find most logically, a wonderful park and garden.

The school itself is housed in an old mansion and its grounds are kept impeccable and even a little wild around the edges. Sycamore trees twist their grey torsos from orange-brown dirt and manicured lawns. Here is shade and shade always means rest (except for moss and mushrooms).

After sipping from the water fountain, which tastes a bit like stainless steel, and crossing the busy curve of street that does have pedestrian markings that no one pays attention to, passing a stand of pines along an open-air area of yet another apartment structure (these are HLM, government housing, and reflect dilapidation and exclusion but in a choice setting) that at least does not purport to have a fancy name. Just past this, the defunct blackened walking bridge floating stories above ground.

The bridge exists. Rain darkened stone, chunks of once white rock growing beards of moss, terraced limestone, it is mysteriously connected to an equally gothic boarded-up mansion. The house's grounds, the bridge linking a yard to the building, are fenced in, off limits, and above the ground, gently lifted by a hill some fifteen feet above the street. A castle hidden and not revealed on maps, this arc and square is the power source of the district. A western pyramid cropping up in a forgotten corner of Old France.

Under the bridge, it always smells of rain. A taste in the nostrils of fat juicy earthworms. It is dark. The walkway is half-paved, as if it were street, but the passage's curbs are of hewn limestone. There are smears of smashed, bicycle-tracked, stepped-in dogshit. Dried out, it's innocuous. The ever-present moisture, seeping from moss, collecting in pools of rain then spilling into rivulets, reactivates the scent occasionally. There are bunches of leaves from a fall that really never ends, if maybe so then in summer, but with the habitual visits of the mistral, they provide the wind's calling cards. Above the bridge, perhaps it's always raining. The rain bridge leading only to its other sides. An accidental arch.

TRAJECTORY SOUTH

After the mysterious bridge, the intersection it opens up to is a busy T. Heading south is as exciting and animated as going west. To go south is to reach the heart. So we shall.

Sunglass shops (only the finest), clothes stores (from very affordable to not) interspersed with incredible smelling *pâtisseries* and equally odiferous *tabacs* (whatever is desired for a minimal fee), then bars and *glaciers* (sometimes in the same locale), then a stone-paved square surrounded by caged trees and yet another bar, a breathing/relaxing space, the surreal juxtaposition of a lit-up cash machine, sycamores, open blue sky between a wedge of old yellowed and whitewashed edifices, tearings of clouds, and then the street continues.

More clothes stores for men and women. Then a fine *papeterie* with incredible paper (for letter writing – they still do that here). Envelopes, books of contemporary and classical literature, even modern English novels in translation!, and also pens, postcards, notebooks (and how the French, or maybe European, notebooks are so notebooky), manuscript clips, even some toys made of wood, and all the magazines one could desire in two lifetimes.

Then, more clothes stores, more sunglass parlors. At the end of the street (past one more bar and at least two restaurants), there is the chapel. It is bright yellow. It sports a Christ crucified, in dark brown wood (one wishes for mahogany), overlooking a bare courtyard with a few sycamores on the edges. Pigeons gather here more than people ever do, but like the people who do, they don't attend mass either. This place is so open and alone.

Out front, on the square, a bus stops occasionally.

There is also a telephone booth to the side of the chapel. The house of worship is the recognizable southern terminus of Mazargues. The neighborhood behind is devoid of tree life. It resembles a factory made into apartments, enlivened only by brightly painted shutters (blue, yellow, green, pink) and by children playing soccer on its concrete and stone fields. Behind the neighborhood fifteen-foot-high walls rise. They conceal a cemetery.

This end of the district, really the beginning of these who enliven it, is a type of French Italy. A Mediterranean in a nutshell – a little stark, but completely alive and colorful. Better than anywhere in the U.S. It is southern and a little gothic, or Romanesque. A very good place to visit on a regular basis, to live in and discover (if only the opportunity existed!), and to enjoy what it has to offer and what one can bring to it: a cigarette and solitude.

Mazargues, continued

Down the other spur of the district, Avenue de la Concorde, one is snug in a bourgeois dream of France. There are more bakeries, fruit stands, meat shops, and houses in between these places and behind them, rising hauntingly into the air, some of which are emblazoned with the golden brass plaques of doctors, lawyers, dentists – the upper crust.

Originally constructed as apartemented living structures, they have in more recent times been maisonette-ed into villa-type residences with hidden courtyards, more than one living level (sometimes three and even four), secret garden walls, by the assurance of monied money.

The street itself is lined with a few caged trees, fewer than on its other axis. On the sidewalk there is hardly enough room to walk, considering the amount of people coming and going, always impossibly beautiful, too beautiful to be moms these women pushing baby strollers; there are fashion shops and hair salons, some bars frequented by an older set that feature cheap *pastis* and always the beer of choice Stella Artois (the prescribed chemical mix for an impassioned game of *pétanque*). There's a solitary electronics store that charges substantially more than any of the local chains ever would, but the secret is they offer much better service. There's a magazine stand that features the mundane weekly press: *Paris Match, L'Express,* a sometimes explicit comic called *Charlie Hebdo,* and of course great girlie magazines. The interesting note to this magazine stand is that the owner's dog looks like a gigantic long-haired muppet, ill-bathed but friendly, unchained and unleashed sitting, playing, peeing on the square and always ready to be petted. There's yet another *papeterie* where one can buy the usual stuff plus little plastic toys and tons of foreign, exotic candies.

In this district, like the fifteen others, one can totally survive without venturing out into the greater world of another district. The difference between one of these self-made, self-sustaining neighborhood units and those in America is this: in France they are naturally occurring and completely distinct from one another.

At the end of Avenue de la Concorde is an obelisk. North of the Egyptian reference point is a southerly extension of the great road the Prado, usually full of a glorious parade of traffic and buses. South going, it heads to a roller coaster of an overpass, and then the flower-blooming outskirts of town and the hills, cliffs, mountains beyond.

Just east of the obelisk, past the giant, American-style gas station, and beyond the small sandwich and fresh oyster shack, is a fenced-off area teeming with natural wild vegetation, a forest kept within the city. Rumor has it that it's dangerous at night, strewn beer bottles desecrate its entrance, but its wild vegetal life force – pines, scrub shrubs, bamboo, wildflowers, and poppies – promise a park or community garden. An ideal but not yet realized breathing space. No manifest destiny here.

Our lady of the guarD

You see them wherever you go. On Broome Street, Sunday mornings, walking arm in arm. He wears a trench coat and carries a *Times* under his elbow. She's telling him something private and unimportant and hanging onto a leash that harnesses a non-descript mutt. The dog sniffs at every other wad of garbage and stain on the sidewalk. All three are oblivious to the steady drizzle and bare branches of the maples holding down the sidewalks at catty-corner. Or they're on Michigan Avenue drinking steaming cups of coffee out of wax-coated paper cups, smiling and walking slowly over the bridge and looking through its eroding segments to see the green river at standstill. In an early afternoon dusting of snow, they're silent thinking each other's thoughts. Come evening, they're at the beach after sunset. Theirs is the only car in the empty parking lot that has become a gathering point for hungry seagulls. A flick of a lighter illuminates the moving silhouettes of their heads for an instant. Voices from the radio slip out of the window cracked open. The surf churns up foam, empty bottles, cigarette butts, and strands of seaweed on the white stones blackened at their base where they touch water.

The traffic is heavy at this time of night. I wait impatiently on the roadside ready to jaywalk. Soon the soccer stadium will be filling with rowdy coliseum goers. Already, some are racing from their neighborhood bars to get the best parking and seats available. It's obvious who they are not only by the speed at which they're driving these winding streets, but by the local team's song they honk out as they pass the beachside restaurants. *Doot dadoot doot doot doot.*

Because it's winter, the city isn't as crowded as it normally is and that's why I'm out walking tonight. There's a certain edifying solitude in being in prime locations at the wrong time. The almost abandoned bars in skiing towns during long American summers. The barren streets of Phoenix in the searing afternoon sun. Or Los Angeles whenever it rains.

The statue the city has erected at its main intersection points eastwards and gives me my cue. I have an hour to make it up the hill to the cathedral. In my backpack I have all I need for my pilgrimage: a notebook and a bottle of water. The hillside dwellings are painted a salmon color of orange. The adobe walls that attempt to conceal them are lined with pieces of broken bottles of varying hues: green, blue, lacquer brown. I carefully put my hand over one of the points to find that it has been dulled by erosion. The leveling power of the wind is a force in these parts.

The hill's seemingly innocuous elevation of two hundred or so meters has me breathing hard three-quarters of the way up. This terrain, which is semi-arid, has formed steep outcroppings of calcite on which the city clings. The landscape is more like desert than temperate zone, but it is well-concealed by pines that spring from anywhere the dusty soil has gathered. There's a garden of wild vegetation bounded by yuccas. It's hard not to continue up the path without looking towards Golgotha. I pass a woman in a fur coat carrying a bag of oranges and she says something about the wonderful view that awaits me. Her hair is dyed with henna and she descends the hill in high heels.

The Moorish spires of the cathedral reach into a blinding sky. They are infused with black stains of gunfire that the Germans left when they attempted to take the citadel. As a matter of pride, the locals let it be known that this part of the country has never been under a Teutonic yoke. Every crack and fissure of the edifice highlighted by a dark erosive effect of rainwater which emphasizes its age and longevity. From a distance, it looks like the walls are growing hair.

When I reach the hilltop, it is surprising to see a group of older Arabs are the only visitors. The men dressed in grey jackets with their white chechias. The women in resplendent djellabas lined in gold lamé, walking up the stairs slowly because of their swollen ankles. When they reach the top piazza, myself steps behind, they look at the sea and point out towards the clouds where Algeria might be. Or Morocco. Perhaps Tunisia. An Egyptian ocean liner steadily crosses the water in between the islands of the bay. It is from the great height that the labyrinth of the city becomes apparent. The tight matrix of red-tiled, concrete buildings below us is beginning to make sense.

There is a couple on the highest viewpoint holding each other and speaking quietly. They are unaware of the futility of traffic and the ships bellowing their horns as they slowly maneuvere into port. The two are awaiting what is theirs this evening – the sun falling into the sea.

Once I enter the cathedral, I no longer wonder why believers of another faith would tour this temple. The singing of monks piped in on tiny, modern, concealed speakers adds to the liminal effect. The ornate interior diffuses such a small irony.

It is more of an art gallery: there are paintings hung on the wall, mobiles of wooden ships strung from the vaulted ceiling, and mosaics of the most stunning colors looking down at a few quiet meditators. The paintings, from what I can make out, were done by locals who had been in some perilous circumstance and, with the grace of divine intervention, survived to tell their stories. Some were done by children. There is a painting of a downed Sopwith Camel with its pilot lying dazed over the target symbol on the wing and a radiant virgin watching over the scene. Heaven in the upper right-hand corner.

Another is of a cat flung to the side of the road by a car, yet miraculously alive, the red tag of its tongue sticking out. There are paintings of clipper ships on stormy seas; of bus crashes in the country; invalids with smiling faces in the hospital. All have the virgin looking over them arrayed in colors of glory.

The whispering of a barely audible voice brings me back from my momentary trance. A little, bent-over woman in the front pews garners my attention. She is busy saying the rosary. When I see the babushka covering her head, I know who it is. I even know her name. Angèle.

I am a long unknown relative of hers – her sister's grandson – and I had found her name in the address book of my grandmother's years ago. I called her just two days ago and explained as best I could who I was, and since I was in this part of the country, I would like to meet her. It is a mystery why someone related to me might be in a country so far from the wilds of Northeast Europe from where the legacy of my line has come. She agreed to my visit and is now patiently awaiting my arrival, steeped in a faith I don't share.

"Hello Madame, let me introduce myself . . ." I begin. She says my name and embraces me.

"You are the spitting image of your mother. It is so good to finally meet you."

I help her up and offer to take her to lunch in the cafeteria nearby but she refuses and tells me that we will have lunch at her place not too far from here.

On the bus ride to her house, she points out to me the houses of neighbors and people she knows. There is the mansion of a Christian Lebanese general who is seeking asylum in the city. The relatively ornate house is guarded by militiamen and is severed from the streets by heavy, moveable iron barricades. It leans on a crag at the sea's edge. There is the apartment of Edward who lost his arm in the war and who comes over on Thursday nights to drink whiskey and play cards. There is where Lorraine lives with her three sisters, all who cook meals for the nuns in the Orthodox convent. Angèle gives the city that keeps to itself behind bright green shutters and blue-tiled addresses a personality.

Her house is a tiny affair that is really more garden than living quarters. She apologizes for it being winter hence the absence of the carnations and gladiolas that regularly surround the place. Inside I am greeted by her son, decades older than I, and a lethargic black cat named Fishbone.

She makes her son, Aldo, and me some soup as if we both are regular visitors who come daily for lunch, while she tinkers around the kitchen and sings a tune under her breath. Aldo is amazed by my presence and asks me many questions. We eat our meal and tell our stories between mouthfuls of soup, then bread, then fish, then salad, then cakes. When the food finally stops, she sits down next to me and simply smiles. I ask her how she got here and why. She begins by saying, "Oh, that old story, well, all right . . ."

'When I was a little girl, about fifteen or sixteen, I worked on a farm. I was in charge of the daily chores, you know, watering the chickens and the ducks, taking hay to the cows, collecting eggs, feeding the goats, combing the horses' manes. There was another worker there named Gregor who was of the marrying age and who was, although I didn't know it at the time, seeking me as his prospect. He wasn't an ugly man but he was large and burly and he had lost an eye when a stubborn mule decided to kick him in the head rather than move.

'One day this Gregor with one eye wanted to help me get the hay for the cows. I can remember the day because it had been raining like the dickens for three days, and this day the rain was sparse, like a mist. Thunderheads were rumbling in the distance but the wind was pushing them away from our neck of the woods and the skies were a lighter grey than they had been. It almost looked like day in the daytime.

'Since he wanted to assist me, I let him because haying the cows was not very fun for me. Although I was a strong girl, the hay was scratchy, getting into my blouse and hair, and heavier than you think. He followed me up the ladder to the loft where the hay was stored. We began pushing clumps of it off the loft to the floor and sweating like pigs because it is much warmer at the top of the barn than at the bottom where there are doors. He took off his shirt while I had to stop every few minutes to wipe the sweat from my brows and eyes. I joked with him saying that it must be easier for him to work hard because the sweat could only go into one of his eyes so he shouldn't have to stop as often as I.

'When I turned to acknowledge my bit of humor, I saw him standing there looking at me. Then he quite mechanically pulled at the rope that held his burlap pants on his waist, and let me say, he did not look tired at all. His . . . his . . . his *thing* was straight up like the handle of a pitchfork, of which I first thought it was, and he took me by the arms, breathing like an animal, and threw me into the bundle of hay. I was a young girl and didn't know what was going to happen, although I had an idea of what was taking place.

'Once father had told me to throw ice cold water from the trough on the stray dog who got stuck in a barn cat when I found them both wailing together in the grain house.

'Gregor had much the very same look in his eye as that poor old dog did.

'I said no, no Gregor, don't treat me like an animal of the barn. You can do whatever you like but please go get a blanket, even if it is the old blanket we put under the horse's saddle. The hay and sharp pieces of straw may cut me so and father will ask me about the cuts when I bathe myself in the tub tonight.

'He held me so close that the sweat from his forehead dropped into my eyes, burning my sight. Everything became blurry. He looked at me so deeply that I thought he had passed out with his one good eye open, but I could hear his breath and his tongue stopping in the back of his throat like an arrow being held on a bow about to be unleashed from its quiver.

'After his moment of thought, he agreed but was unable to retie the knot of rope fastened to his pants, so let them fall to his ankles and hobbled down the ladder. He took the blanket from a peg on the wall and hopped up the ladder without even using his hands.

'When he was almost to the loft, with my bare feet I pushed the ladder as far out as I could. Gregor then grabbed it with his hands and, on the ladder, stood straight up and down.

'With much exertion, he managed to balance on the ladder, I thought that it might fall back onto the loft and I would be raped, maybe become pregnant, and have to marry this awful man and this terrible future played out like a moving picture in my mind. But when his pants tore in half from between his ankles and he looked down, the ladder toppled backwards and he fell to the ground on his back.

'I yelled for help and Poppa came into the barn. I said that Gregor fell because I accidentally pushed the ladder away from the loft with a stroke of the pitchfork. Gregor was moaning – lying in the dirt with the rags of his pants around his ankles – and we never discussed the event ever again.

'It turned out that Gregor had only broken his shoulder bone and some ribs and would return to our farm in the fall when he was better. I knew that something terrible would happen to me if we were both to be working in a field beyond a call to the house. Then I knew I had to leave.

'Your grandmother had saved enough money to take the boat to America and before she left, she gave me the name of a family living in Paris who had posted a work notice at the University. These people needed a maid to keep the house and care for the children so I wrote them a letter and they offered me the job.

'So I was off to Paris. It was a much better life. I lived in a big house and would only have to go to the street to find milk and the finest cheeses and bread, and good bread at that. The man I worked for was a government official and paid me well and the children were darling and I was very happy. Then the Germans came and took the city and the family I worked for had to leave. Without an explanation, they told me I should get out of the city and go far away to be safe. They were moving to another country, but they wouldn't tell me where to ensure my own safety. I packed what little I had, and with a friend of mine who was a cook in a restaurant that the Germans shut down, went to the government office to find work somewhere else.'

At this point, Angèle's speech begins to wax more and more into an accent and it becomes harder for me to understand her story. Aldo helps me out by translating phrases here and there. I notice her eyes begin to gloss over with a wetness as she speaks, staring at an embroidered pattern on the table cloth.

'It so happened that the Germans briefly were in control of the hospital here in the southern part of the country. When they left, the Italians took over but soon abandoned it as the war changed to different theaters, and so for reasons beyond my knowledge, the British took control. We were offered jobs doing the laundry and whatnot but we had to hitchhike down here from Paris. In between Paris and here, a farmer dropped us off in a city, I can't remember the name, but it was large enough to have a zoo, and because he knew someone who worked there, he suggested that we stay there until he could arrange a ride for us to reach the hospital.

'We used the cloth bags that carried what little luggage we could take as blankets and we made our beds in an empty cage that previously was an exhibit of wolves from the forests of Bavaria. It still smelled of them and their droppings were lying all around like loaves of moldy bread. I barely slept that night because of the noise the rats made. I kept waking on the hour thinking that there was a solitary wolf they had forgotten to remove, hiding in the corner, ready to attack us at any moment.

'In the morning we were awakened by men's voices and a loud noise like the sound of sawing. It seemed that one of the miniature horses had died and the workers were cutting it into rations. I saw the body of this lovely creature disassembled as if it were a broken toy, its bloody hindquarters leaning up against a wooden fence.

'The same farmer that took us to the town gave us a ride to this city after we both did a day's worth of chores and paid him some money on top of it. I remember that ride through the country, through the farmland that turned from rows of corn into lines of black, wiry grapevines. It was the first time that I was able to see such an amount of land. Green hills that bleached to white. It became my country.

'When we finally arrived here, there was a notice posted in the hospital that proclaimed if one could raise a certain amount of money, a visa could be issued to go to America. My dear friend who was younger than I didn't have enough money so I gave her the rest of mine from my days working as a maid and the next day I said my goodbye to her at the port. I have never seen or heard from her again.

'I found an ad for a room for rent at the grocery store and called. The gentleman who was the landlord and recently released from his duty gave me the room, explaining that it would have electricity in a week or so, but despondent as I was, I moved in immediately. I cooked my meals outside using wood and I washed my clothes down the hill in the sea. That room was in the house next door.'

Aldo breaks in saying, "And in that week, he did provide the electricity. The landlord, you see, is my father."

We break out in laughter. But he soon becomes solemn when he explains that his father is quite sick and is staying in the very hospital that was Angèle's passport to freedom. The beginning of her life and the sad chapter that is now unraveling are found at the same location. The hospital is just up the hill overlooking the turquoise Mediterranean.

'We would go to the horse races, even the bullfights when they had them. Or we would just walk along the beach and watch the hills turn orange at day's end. Now they won't even let me bring him meals. And I can only see him for hours a day.'

She begins to cry. It is now dark outside. The features of the Black Madonna hanging near the window can no longer be made out. We exchange addresses. As I prepare for my departure, Angèle offers me a room to stay in but I tell her that I have one rented on the other side of town. I promise that the family in America will make contact as soon as possible and that if there is any assistance I can provide . . .

They both thank me, Angèle gives me a biscuit for my bus ride back and Aldo hugs me as if I am his long-lost son. I don't want to leave but I have to get back to my small room and the family who is renting it to me. I will be leaving the country in a few days.

Fishbone the cat follows me as far as the front gate and makes a sound that sounds like "No" as I close the lock and wave goodbye.

I catch the bus on the top of the hill near the tall hospital building that stands with most of its lights on. The bus is empty except for a couple in the back who hold onto each other as if the destination they long for is sleep. His leather jacket creaks when he moves and she has a delicate silver ring pierced into her nostril. They talk at each stop we come to.

Because you see them everywhere you go. Carrying bread home from the baker's or watching television together in a dimly lit apartment levels above the main street. They travel to foreign countries together or hold jobs in the same office. They talk of vacations they shared in the mountains or times they learned how to ride mopeds along the narrow alleys of the downtown. They share the quotidian intimacies of the day. Their shoes left stepping on each other at the door. Their clothes intertwined in the hamper. A round coffee stain on the pillowcase. Theirs are the secret stories of how they met and fell in love and how they let this love narrate the all too short story of their lives.

When we reach my temporary block of the neighborhood, I signal for a stop. I am the only one left on the route. I still hold the biscuit Angèle gave me in the warm hollow of my pocket. I wonder where the young couple was going. If they live around here, in an apartment, it can't be too far from where I am staying. The doors hiss open and the bus driver turns around. He waves to me and with a wink says, "Until we meet again."

A WALK WITHOUT CÉZANNE

Among the many paintings of Mt. St. Victoire the artist left behind, there isn't one that investigates the mountain up close, to reveal its blatant texture of Provence. At least not myopically. There are his famous views from the Bibémus quarry, scenes from and even of Château Noir, scenes derived out of the randomness of his jauntings through the surrounding fields and meadows. But none of the calcite and limestone itself, the scrub and moss broken like blankets left outside to be shredded by time and the wind. To mention the number of cats killed each year by the invisible cyclones of the mistral, would only be for the sake of cliché. What makes this sacred mountain of Western Civilization a mountain and not but a cliff of land that couldn't reach far enough to overlook the sea, is all a matter of perspective. Its bricks are stained in rainwater like those of skyscrapers in New York dripping in cascades of acidic black. The will to oxidize is pure. Lonely pines left levels below, their trunks gnarled in poses of self-exposure. Even the incomplete writings in color the artist left behind, seemingly faded, yet still easily read by the eye, reveal more than they conceal. Did Cézanne mean for them to be as shielded from the weather as they are? To prevent pictures from the eternity of stone and vegetation from which their colors are ground? The cross of Our Lady erected near one of the summits serves a dual purpose. One

is to mark the height of this mountain's earthly spine, the other:
an unsaid cenotaph.

An intriguE

News arrives today from Les Goudes via the magic of e-mail, an invention that concurrently separates places as it connects them through the telephonic space illusion of instantaneous-ness. Just because your ghost, your thoughts, in electronic form, can be in a spot thousands of miles away, and access to this phantasm is readily available, it makes you all that much farther away.

It turns out that a friend had to walk the length of the village to her cabanon last night due to multiple police cordons: "there was a murder a few cabanons from your old place."

The rumor is that a jealous boyfriend killed his lover before attempting, and failing, to take his own life. A very bizarre, almost American-style scenario, occurring in that tiny place where in two years of tenure I noticed only one mock fisticuffs fight between two men. The other occurrence of any note was, the late afternoon a trawler pulled in a thirteen-foot tuna. At first sight from across the small bay, it looked like a horribly bloated scuba diver.

This murder forces me to think, to do my own reluctant, impotent detective work concerning whom it might have been. So little in France ever changes, especially addresses. What was initially the guts of a planned industrial complex in Les Goudes that developed into the modern port that has now overrun Fos north of the city, was converted into a gigantic, many-tiered adobe birdhouse with one middle row of cabanons, housing a usual cast of characters.

There is Stavros, an old Greek fisherman, who starts his day at seven a.m. He takes a mid-morning goûter, a keep-oneself-going snack at ten a.m. consisting of a bowl of green olives and some type of clear liquor, most likely ouzo. There is an older couple with a tiny dog that comes and make amorous advances to our five times its size German Shepherd. Mousquette is its name. There are younger to middle-aged couples who keep cabanons as summer getaways, bringing with them their well-behaved children. The two or three families obviously know each other well and prove so by lunching and dining together while the children play on inflatable boats in the tiny port, sometimes even causing incoming fishing boats, called pointus, to pause, angrily raising waves, before shutting off their put-putting engines and silently docking. The dinners last well into the darkness of summer evenings. Nights, lit by jovial banter, stars, reflections on the water, candles. It couldn't have happened to these well-adjusted pleasure seekers.

There was, however, a mysterious woman who would greet us whenever we were lucky enough to catch a glimpse of her — the door of her cabanon open while she tidied her digs. She was of local exquisitely handsome Mediterranean stock: rather tall, long chocolate hair, darkly tanned, blue eyes.

Her terrace was exposed to the view from ours, looking diagonally. Being directly in front of her living quarters, her wooden-beam topped patio on the sea looked like a picnic construction I stopped at off Highway 40 in New Mexico, her terrace was on the other side of the walkway stretching in front of the row of cabanons. She would habitually entertain a gentleman here, to dinner and drinks, even further into the evening than the happy families on the southerly side of her seaside escale. Acting as occasional voyeur, as sometimes undeniably all writers must do, I would use the excuse of venturing out onto my hidden terrace to listen to the distinctly American jazz being played live at the bar, just up the rock outcrop, le bar Sunset. This little bistro was a temptation in itself, having everything from food, drink, ice cream, tobacco, an exquisite view on the sea and a private beach, and probably other items if one inquired. I would go out there just to watch her.

If my Madame X is gone now, or whomever it might have been, it doesn't really matter. It's nevertheless very disconcerting. Murder in France is rare, even with the supposed racial tensions of the South. Crimes of passion, on the other hand, might be a legacy that the passions of great food, sun, and nudity engender. Men are sun kings and women are earth goddesses and rather than scandalous adultery, sex is a consuming force that burns like a naturally occurring fire. On the Mediterranean, when love goes bad, it extinguishes itself.

Un-easy access

In America, it is so simple to get anything whenever it is desired. Even if it isn't wanted, it can still be attained, and usually this is the case. Pancakes for dinner. Twenty-four hours a day hamburgers cooking. There was once even a breakfast soda marketed. Generally speaking, this modus operandi makes life easier, not better, and people get confused about the two.

In France, there is no grocery shopping to be done on a Sunday. There aren't any open. Acquisitions must be planned and the daily routine is determined by what needs to be done based on a culturally developed window of availability. One must know exactly which *pâtisserie* to go to exactly when to get the freshest bread within a four-block accumulation of local, family-run bakeries. It is the same with the *boucherie,* the corner fruit markets, and the myriad small groceries, named Casino. It's a constant gamble.

There is no all-night anything, except for roads. The evening is a sacred time more for taking strolls along the beach or settling into giant tables of many-course meals and unplugged and respiring wine bottles. Sometimes dinner isn't served until nine p.m. And there's always the sport of people watching because the French do not lock themselves up at night. It is when they truly begin to be alive.

Nights, and even non-siesta hours, are geared to the ultimate enjoyment of every minute. One proof might be the fact that video stores close at eight p.m. There are natural, timed quotas of temptation. There would never be anything as preposterous as a drive-in liquor store.

One ritualistic way to celebrate the unraveling of evening's cloak in Marseille is to bring a freshly wood oven-fired pizza to the city's rocky coastline and enjoy it with a bottle or two of wine. Alcohol is not prohibited in public places – the French couldn't maintain such a hypocrisy. Consequently, there isn't an abuse of the freedom. Unlike the dwelling place of liberty that is the U.S., the French enjoy greater freedoms of not a libertine vein, but those of the art of intoxicating the brain with the best life has to offer.

Waves hugging the warm, sandy shoulder of *la plage du Prado*, stars overhead, lovers in an isolated cove of stone, fish observable in the clear blue water meditating into sleep, the yap of a dog free of any concept of a leash as the city tucks itself into a highly bearable numbness of yet another perfect sunset as the mountains that surround eerily glow standing sentinel over this divine form of day's end. An enchantment known in very few other dreamworlds.

Rêverie

In a dream, the city awakens. Pigeons coo in abandoned storied buildings that will in no time considering the surrounding geology open into new restaurants featuring *tapas,* or maybe morph into summer abodes of the rich and totally infamous, or they'll become artist studios without the luxury of hot running water. Their shutters are painted in archaic green and aren't at the least concerned about their flaked, dilapidated, shaggy personal appearance. It's good enough that they even open and ever so rarely close. Yellowness seeps into streets that will be washed clean come dawn by men in brightly colored, orange or green or blue, jumpsuits who have not found anything better to do with their lives but smoke and talk and walk through these canyons of history and human inhabitants who think nothing of emptying old dishwater or recently filled ashtrays onto the people streaming sidewalks below, whenever a purifying urge comes along. In evening's silence it is never quiet. Always a lonely moped blurting home. A stray *deux chevaux* lost among dark, drunken roads. The pigeons dropping an afternoon's spoils of tossed out breads, oversee that paradise is a quotidian thing. Pigeons, who'll never leave their self-made, self-claimed rooks and nooks of buildings, try to find a convincing reason to leave. Rather, they preen.

INCIDENTAL

French doors, in France, are *porte-fenêtres* – door-windows, and this conceptual rendering means more than it could anywhere else. If one is so lucky to have them opening onto a terrace, these liminal beings dictate one's life. That is to say, in the morning or evening – the outside world – its temperature, smells, sounds, is a constant entity worth visiting/meditating on.

To open them, their handles must be first twisted, then raised, which is akin to the sacramental opening of a large secular tabernacle. They close, aligning top and bottom hooks to meeting catches, above, below, and in the middle. They are escape hatches into the realms of pigeons and marauding magpies, gardens of potted plants, and Islamic renderings of tiled floors and cool, shady places lit by sunlight or stars.

French doors are usually paned with ancient wavy glass that when closed reflects light in oceanic currents and provides a skewed view of what is beyond. They are ever so romantic when hung with curtains, stately when adorned with peeling paint, and in their larger than people statures, remind us that what occurs outside of them is much more relevant than the human machinations that unfold within their view.

View from a
solitary locatioN

The view from opened French doors on a two-tiered terrace in a remote, unremarkable spot in a southerly *banlieue* of an oft-disparaged city is surprisingly not of ruin, the drug-addicted, homeless, or the forgotten, as most of the current guidebooks lending insight will have you read. Rather, from this solitary perch, Western, desert-like buttes stretching into giant steps colored in weeds of pine, escalate to the cloud-ridden south. Blue, flatness of sea that is merely a tangent of promise. A hill adorned in the north with a cathedral that looks like a decoration on an ornate wedding cake. Beyond it, forested hillsides ending in sharp peaks of green and whiteness and another church-topped promontory in the southeast. Endless cumulus arranged orderly by the heat of the day, blue sky that suggests North Africa and Spain, surreptitious views into other apartments, houses, villas, bars with *boules* courts, trees and incalculable Mediterranean greenery, schools, neighborhoods where beautiful people live lives that will never need qualification. Streets that anonymously wind into well-worn labyrinths, parks and verdant corners that beckon exploration with glass of *pastis* in hand, and the strangest of all feelings, an overall erotic beckoning that says: you will never know me fully but you are welcome to explore, feel, sense, touch.

Marseille is the erogenist's playground.

CITADEL UNWINDING

In 1494 Queen Isabella I of Spain calculated Marseille to be the exact center of the world. Perhaps based on faulty maps (the Sephardim of Portugal made superior ones at the time) or considering the city's reputation of containing varied, exotic peoples from endless corners of the earth set in a romantic, otherworldly, oriental topography, she wasn't, judging by modern-day standards, all that off the mark. The sun, ever clear and blinding, has the ability to play tricks on one's perception. One place the city opens up to the gaze of all interested newcomers is upon the grand stone cascade of steps at the Gare St. Charles train station.

Its grandiosity is a baroque hallucination of the early nineteen twenties. The view from the top is purely Borgesian – a labyrinth beckons below that is of Istanbul's degree of ominous complexity. Clouds parrying off the sea conceal butte-like mountaintops far, white, and ghostly arid in the distance. Immediately below, spires only vaguely suggesting cathedrals do nothing other than spire; grimy commercial and residential buildings spawn clones of themselves that remain somehow subtly distinct in angle and haphazard construction of terrace, window, and orange-tiled roof.

The din is remarkable: buses letting farts of fuel and hissing air brakes; people speaking, yelling, cursing, laughing (it's tempting to calculate how much public laughter, comparatively, occurs in the U.S.); cars zooming dangerously through dangerous intersections, which is truly an illusion of proximity and the lack of trust in superior European driving skills. Intersections don't exist, rather there is an instinctual placing of traffic lights.

For a truly adrenaline-producing exercise, one can rent a car in any big city in France, to test, firstly, one's mettle and then one's driving skills. It's no malapropism that racing is termed *pilotage.* For driving fast in France is vitally linked to the sport of racing, as ingrained to them as baseball and basketball are to Americans. A note of advice: they always have the home court advantage. If any type of mishap occurs, demur apologetically.

Music wafts and wails from local bars on the Boulevard d'Athènes. This street is the one that takes a weary traveler from the train station's steps to the famous Canebière and the walk is characteristically Marseillais: hardly touristy, lined with trees and humanity inhabiting small *épiceries* tucked under natural color and man-made striped blue awning of shadiness. The street is towered over by indistinct but gloriously aged apartment buildings, leading one nowhere remarkable except past a bookstore, Gilbert, that houses English classics in its sidewalk wooden cart bins. There's even more inside.

As it gently slopes down into the wild, Byzantine heart of the city, Boulevard d'Athènes is colored by ever increasing small "sandwicheries" and relatively few pornographic cinemas sunken back into alleyways and haunches of grey buildings.

Nowhere in the world is it easier to transition from one's personal world to the world at large. Nowhere in the world, leaving from America, can one so quickly walk into an antithesis.

Nowhere in the world can one find oneself in the heart of its aptly named, yet still unrecognized, *centre ville.*

Views from l'estaque

As a focal point for the occurrence of modern art, thanks to the likes of Cézanne, Braque, Dufy, Matisse, Marquet, Pissarro, the small coastal village of l'Estaque is a place perfect for a Sunday stroll. Now, the modern port and docks of Fos encroach, but local charm still reigns.

L'Estaque looks out onto the sea, *pieds dans l'eau,* feet in the water as the French say, and it is remarkable in that it is one of the few, if not only, places one can purchase a *chi chi.* It's a beignet deep fried and covered in sugar and topped with either chocolate, Nutella, or real whipped cream. It's akin to a gigantic churro that's soft as a pillow and is instantaneously filling.

Marquet's terrace, or a place very like it still exists with a panoramic view of the bay of Marseille, the massif Marseilleveyre cutting into the sea like a damascened scimitar, and the view is available to any pedestrian. L'Estaque is a place that hasn't been contaminated by the rich and infamous as such a location would be, years back, if this were southern California. In a nightmarish hallucination, one can see Circle K signs dotting the coastline.

There isn't much to do or see in l'Estaque and graciously there aren't any trendy shops selling worthless baubles. The town remains what it will always be: a contemplative relic of Mediterranean Europe that is conducive only to outings of boating, strolling, or of a picnicking variety. Just past L'Estaque, going north and west, the coastal cliffs resemble lunar deserts abloom with Aleppo pines. There is a romanesque, arched bridge that beckons the traveler to stop under its architecture. A railroad track tunnels into the small, rugged mountains and lends an air of the American West.

Down the coastal range Chaîne des Etoiles are the dream villages of Carry-le-Rouet and Sausset-les-Pins. These hamlets are attained by roads that literally drop from a plateau to steep cliffsides bordering the sea. It is difficult to park in these villages and the residents prefer it that way. The *calanques* these lucky people inhabit contain crystal clear water, placid tides, relaxed octopuses snoozing among submerged breakers, beaches with stones of every hue of a painter's palette, and an endless mind-lulling whir of cicadas doing what they do best – mate and sing.

HALLOWEEN

This resolutely Anglo-Saxon feast is becoming more popular in France because the French will celebrate anything. It's in their blood. Halloween translates well because it incorporates equal elements of the masque, the fête, and the carnival. Having assisted its introduction one pleasantly nippy October night in Marseille, this is how that hallowed eve went.

We invited a crowd of interested friends who were more than willing to dress the part. They appeared as devils in fishnet stockings, corpses attired in tuxedos, Frankensteins with slicked hair, Draculas adept at dancing to rap, angels in ballerina tutus, and even biker folk.

Not having a *sou* to spend on an ornate costume, I went as a serial killer, armed with a spooky white theatrical face of a mask (I believe it was meant to represent a clown) and a large plastic butcher knife. Not exactly the life of the party. I had to many times explain the American fascination with serialized death, a very patriotic pastime it seems, and this left the participants a bit uneasy.

We began the evening with the requisite bobbing for apples, which we really couldn't historically explain, other than a tipsy re-telling of the headless horseman tale, which obviously lead to the intoduction of a jack o' lantern.

French fruit markets do carry a type of *courge* that resembles a small, flattened pumpkin, but it is nearly impossible to carve a face into its stunted attempt at pumpkin-ness. We drew evil faces on these little foreign squashes and backlit them with candles which utterly perplexed, but interested, the party-goers.

After a prolonged bout of *apéritif* consumption, we decided to march through the streets of Marseille in costume. A friend had even made papier-mâché skulls from which he would scoop out a makeshift concoction of tomato paste and macaroni: home-made brains.

Our entourage, the only one of the evening we were aware of, loosely stringing past clubs and bars, one aptly named Le Vamping, completely stumped the residents and business owners of the usually quiet, subsiding into evening, downtown.

I made the mistake of wandering into a "bar Américain" (local hub of prostitution) adorned in my mask and wielding, what looked like under dim red lights, a real knife. The women inside screamed as I was amazed at their completely appropriate attire. I invited them to our get-together at a local establishment on the port and let them know that initially they would have to pay in what could turn out to be a lucrative business outing.

When we arrived at the nightclub that acted as hosts to our party – a bar/restaurant that had agreed to provide free food if we bought ample drink, the gorgeous bartendresses were nonplussed. Between beers, and with a wink, and big tips, they would fire off a round of free drinks. Very congenial. There was a table with of all things: chips and salsa, fried *fruits de mer* including kalamari, and as if they had planned for the arrival of us pilgrims, a cold salad featuring kernels of corn.

The night unfolded in an environment of loud music, scantily clad women, eager men, tidbits of food whenever required by long sessions of wine drinking with an occasional smoke. Those tourists and locals who walked past the walls of window were too reserved to come in.

There was dancing. A carnival of souls. Best of all, there was no candy.

All too soon, at about three in the morning, our disguises were shorn so that we could get to know one another better. There was more dancing and kissing than there should have been, maybe. I found the leader and originator of our fête dancing on the bar with three acolytes of the opposite sex.

It was the best Halloween ever. A celebration that will undoubtedly be transformed by the French into their own Mardi Gras, only better.

BUSES OF MASSILIA

If there's a way to best experience the hypercomplex, difficult to get to know, and deeply secretive city, it must be on the buses and entwined metro lines.

Coming into the city from the south, as not many people do, from the sleepy hamlet of Les Goudes, it is the rare 20 that ambles along the winding coast. This bus runs a fraction of the time the others do and is mostly used by hikers and pleasure seekers leaving the confines of the city. When on the 20, a smaller than usual bus made mostly of windows, its passengers "ooooh" and "aahhhh" most of the way and can't help but stand up to participate in the mountain, cliff, island, and sea views. It ends in Callelongue, where the road also ends. In this tiny *calanque* village, hemmed in by cliffside and pine, there is an excellent pizzeria, a bay and tiny beach, and trail heads that take one on many routes to the great uninhabited beyond.

The 20 originates at Madrague – a bus stop in front of an ancient chapel. Inside the chapel that is always open and normally unvisited, there is a huge aquarium of exotic fish. This is the fisherman's house of prayer, although one hasn't been under its cross-topped roof probably in decades, where prayers are logged in for the men out on the seas earning a living. It is a most elegant and odd relic of the past built into the hillside of Mount Rose. One can wait for the bus in the chapel's rock-carpeted courtyard overhung with scent rich pines. Probably it's the best bus stop in the world.

And then the 19 arrives. What is distinct about it is that it is an intimate line. It is always manned or womanned by a Marseillais(e) with golden skin, dark hair, facial features of unusual attractiveness. The bus driver, who will often have but a few riders will engage any or all of them in conversation. It's a lonely, windswept route lined by foothills and mountains, unbelievable views of rocks and waves just beyond the coast, initially with a stretch of lower income cabin-like houses built on a cliffside – looking like a community of people who worship paranormal roofs. What a gig for a city worker to get, driving this line.

The driver will be interested where in the city you are going because he or she will have family there or friends. The driver will describe recent out of the ordinary passengers. When the bus is waiting its precise minute of departure (by which you as rider should set your watch) he or she will enjoy an illegal on the bus cigarette or even sip at a beverage concealed under the spacious dashboard.

Paper bus tickets are no longer used because they would be stamped with such an invisible amount of ink that they could easily be used again and again. The change to an electronically charged card/scanning system hasn't curbed the insidious arrival, at any time, of the team of RTM monitors. Usually it's a collection of three men, women, or combination, wearing their characteristic blue windbreakers. They are dropped off near any given bus stop by car, and they emerge, out of the blue, at the bus stop too soon for any free rider perpetrator to get off the bus. When they're picked up, only the front doors on the bus are opened, thus foiling any attempt at quick escape. A rolling venus flytrap.

It is either a terrifying, embarrassing, or annoying interruption that is never gladly welcomed especially in the hot, un-air-conditioned summer months. One has to reproduce one's card and be subjected to this personal questioning of integrity. The process is always met with a lowering of the shoulders, the general bodily portrayal of the motif of "a sinking feeling", and a loud, forceful exhalation of breath. This gesture is expected by everyone involved. Wouldn't be the same without it. *phhhffffffffffooooooooooooooooooooooo* . . .

This minor inconvenience soon becomes an investigative foray when one is caught. The rest of the riders are treated to the drama of the violators barrage of excuses for not having a paid-up card. Technical malfunction on the card's part, or the scanning machine's accuracy, is the most popular wheedling. If caught, it results not only in the ignominy of being caught in public, having your feathers ruffled in stuffy plein air, but a weighty fine of two hundred and fifty francs.

The trip from Madrague to its first point of connection, Rond Point du Prado, is a sensual dream voyage. One passes the Italianate alleys of La Madrague de Montredon without a hint of the tiny port and restaurant just behind its cluttered rues.

On the other side of the street there is government housing that produces often the strangest and most exotic passengers waiting outside of the many-storied shoebox of a building. Perhaps there is migration from the poor dwellings across it, resembling those of Mexico's Pacific coast. Surely, the seaside homes, though looking dangerous and forlorn, must be more habitable.

Continuing past the park that is the Pastré, a château once owned by a wealthy Russian émigré, now housing a ceramic museum. Even if faïence doesn't at all sound interesting, it's worth the few franc entry fee just to walk around the stately mansion, to walk up its stone stairways, and to peer at the sea and pine top view from its small upstairs windows.

After winding through quaint, newer neighborhoods, you arrive at Pointe Rouge. It's a secret seaside (not to locals) destination that features some of the city's best dessert shops, bakeries, and beachside haunts that are slightly overpriced but well worth the views and atmospheres of blue neon. The beach of Pointe Rouge is populated by a large crowd of those who actually use its waters for sports and frolicking. A very young crowd is attracted by its bay-like location and cafés and glaceries where the main dish featured is ice cream. Needless to say, it also attracts a host of people watching people.

The beach is bordered by a walkway and wall that rises some thirty feet above the sand. Men like soldiers guarding the coast gaze at lunchtime fantasies below. At beach level, there is also a row of *cabanons* built in to the retaining wall, two bona fide restaurants, and a major wind surfing port of departure. The beach itself is pure, finely eroded sand with an uncharacteristic lack of urchin-filled rocks in the shallow water.

All the temptations that make life worth living in such a small spot on an unassuming stretch of coast. It's a great place to be human.

Archipelago inconnU

This rocky point and beach of polished stones is a little south of Pointe Rouge, hidden in a more remote nook of the coast. It features long stretches of reefs that jut into the sea. They can be traversed when the tide allows. The rocky beach is backed by an even steeper staircase and higher wall and another walkway for the lonely to pause on bicycle rides to peer at those sunning themselves below. Perhaps this place is a bike riding/viewing destination.

South of the tiny crescent-shaped beach there are staircases built into rock that lead to large houses that straddle the overhanging plateau. Beyond these often gated staircases of concrete is a rocky *calanque* that is for the most part impassable, or looks too dangerous for the faint of heart to cross, especially so when the mistral is blowing three-foot waves. After the gorge, there is another world of pure rock and sea, a stone and mineral embankment of torturous landscape pitted with secret caves.

The texture of this larger archipelago resembles the topography of a distant planet. There are small, pointed mountain ranges of spikes, blades of limestone sea teeth that can shred any type of footwear, or at least do great damage. There are pools that form and sometimes contain sea snails, tiny crabs, and bizarre crystallizations of salt.

On the hidden archipelago, one is sheltered from any signs of civilization. It's a strange continuity of rock and water, desolate but inviting. Fishermen wearing hip boots sometimes fish its shores. Caves formed by consuming forces of wind and wave offer a little shelter from the midday sun. Like columns of a fallen temple, this place is nature in spectacular ruin. No plant life even attempts to stay for too long.

Swimming off the archipelago offers the snorkeler an underwater city of rocks, sunken column-like structures and accretions of dead sea life, schools of curious fish, all kinds and sizes of hermit crabs, a type of crab that wears a wig of seaweed which is startling on first encounter as it appears from nowhere with its claws as big as a human fist. There are purpley green anemones and sandy stretches of submerged beach that encompassed with sea grass and piles of cliff-fallen stone, suggest the outskirts of Atlantis.

The remoteness, within the city, of this forgotten, singular niche offers one a pure, simple, easy escape from the civilization that has endured around it for eons. Of course, when the waves kick up, the sea urchin-bedecked reefs and rocks can be very unsettling, as I found myself pincushioned on them in one strong current of bad judgment. They are a delicacy to eat but are treacherous to pet, greet, or touch in any way.

The sting of an urchin is closest to, in my experience, the prick of being attacked by a jumping cholla cactus of the Sonoran desert. The urchin's needles, like those of the cactus, lodge in the skin and remain there visibly in the form of tiny dots, long after contact has ceased. Soon after the skin swells a little and a speckled bruise tattoos the inflicted body part. Sometimes a single urchin needle makes its way into the flesh like a most excruciating splinter. It sinks in further if you attempt to pry it out. The lingering pain is only unbearable if pressure is applied to the area lodged with *épines.* If a swimmer is so unlucky to step on one, his or her gait will assuredly change for the next month or so.

Dredging oneself up from the sea after hours of shell collecting, marine life observation, and the hopeful search for sea caverns, the beach of the archipelago offers an audience of sunbaked, glistening bodies wholly uninterested in your arrival. The sea closes the parting that spews you forth, quietly, behind.

Past the sandwich shop l'Américano which is the moniker for a type of ham and cheese sandwich with tomatoes with mustard on French bread, Michelangelo's, or rather Cantini's reproduction of, David beckons you down the corniche.

Marseille's David is regularly vandalized, though that's too harsh a word. He has been spotted wearing a cloth fig leaf; once even a thong swimsuit. He has proudly worn the hometown soccer team's jersey in the form of it spray painted on his upper body. He once wore a gigantic styrofoam ten-gallon hat. Occasionally there are messages, or tattoos, decorating his butt cheeks. It is never quite known how his stark, stoic appearance will be altered by the youth of the day.

His looming presence provides a weird juxtaposition that somehow makes sense overlooking the beach of the Prado where men and women congregate around open air showers to bathe their bodies free of salt in front of a well-mannered, interested public. The greens surrounding the outdoor showers are popular picnic spots.

Bus 19 then veers eastward up a Parisian boulevard lined by old mansions of old money and French banks. There are pushcart oyster bars under the shade of plane trees on the way to the city's southerly hub.

Rond Point du Prado is a rowdy bus and underground metro stop due to its location adjacent to the soccer stadium, recently renovated for the World Cup. Behind the escalator and bus drop-off point, there is a pleasant park. Around the circle, the *rond* of the point, there are cafés and sandwich carts (one featuring Greek fare) and many benches and trees. It's a place to stop for a moment and re-vitalize before entering the traffic-filled, exuberantly alive *centre ville.*

The underground metro connection (there are above ground ones in the northeastern section of the city) here is host to fast food-like *patisseries* that make its confines smell of freshly baked croissants. This fringe benefit keeps the RTM guard dogs always alert and a little hungry. There's a hungry dreaminess in their eyes.

NOTES ON BUS ETIQUETTE

1) The young man who jumps on the bus without inserting a payment card, adorned with blaring walkman, cigarette butt tucked into mouth corner, avoiding eye contact with anyone except himself in the window's reflection should be both tolerated and ignored. Especially when the older woman who lives to correct others' behavior begins speaking.

2) If there is a lack of empty seats, one immediately evacuates his or her seat when an older rider mounts. The older rider chooses or declines the invitation to sit. The evacué(e) is respected by all evinced by an irregular ripple of nodding heads and requisite smiles.

3) The presence of the bus driver should be acknowledged by a *bonjour* or *bonsoir*. If the prospective rider ran to the bus stop, causing the driver to halt acceleration, or, in the most egregious case, a halt and re-opening of the doors, the tardy rider must thank the driver repeatedly while voicing a *vous êtes gentil(lle)*.

4) That the plastic seating is arranged 2 X 2 in rows of two, if one is seated on the outside of such a configuration, he or she is always expected to offer the inside seat to a rider of female persuasion.

5) On crowded buses bodily contact is allowable especially between attractive members of the opposite sex. To a degree.

TarzaN

He wears a jacket, brown black and white houndstooth, a light tan, almost off-white shirt underneath, matching brown pants, grey shoes. The clothes are from Emmaüs, a French version of the Salvation Army. The lines worn into his forehead, around his eyes suggest some sixty-odd years of natural furrowing. His hair is white and grey, combed back Cesar Romero-style and is always kept oiled. He walks the neighborhood singing and wishing well to everyone he sees even if he knows them not. He is never without a tale to tell, a recollection of you, or someone who looks like you, when you both were much younger, happier. He's always been around. He wants to shake your hand and, even, hug. He wants to make contact because no one loves him or probably ever will. Maybe someone did once. Although he's known by all in the *arrondissement,* that sleepy collection of concrete walls, holly bushes, some walls and gates, the corners overhung with sweet smelling mimosa branches, no one knows where he lives. He was born in Algeria, a place of which he never speaks. He is charming, a nuisance if he spots you when you're rushed, but he won't remember the fact that you surreptitiously crossed the street with your head hung low. He always smells vaguely of cheap aftershave and ripe figs. His hands are smooth and warm. He is the local drunk who will dedicate and sing any song to you and only you.

Lost and FounD

There is a house, what I consider to be a "house" but what is really a *premier étage* – a large apartment that is located above shops that line the street. There is nothing above this type of dwelling, no third or further floors. The door is on the street which opens to a hallway with a long winding stairway leading to the loft-like multi-roomed residence.

In one of the rooms (a total of nine) there is a door behind the door. This door has not been opened for thirty years. The room itself is a monumental coffer, a reliquary, what the family refers to as a *fouillis* (a mess). It exists in a similar form in probably thousands, tens of thousands of incarnations, just outside the realm of history.

In America, one might have an attic, a cubbyhole, but in France an entire, once livable room is preserved for the past's relics because days gone by deserve their own private enclave. A chest of priest's vestments in perfect condition from, no one knows for sure, 1920s? Newspapers in yellow bundles that detail world wars and the deaths of presidents. Rotten, crumble-apart communion hosts. Boxes of dolls from many childhoods of at least three generations of women. Life-size babies with disconcertingly human eyes and coifs of horsehair. A tin container containing medallions of religious belief: blue jewel Marys, crosses with green serpents entwined, other crosses with ornately tortured Jesuses in tears of blood, and simple Celtic-like crosses aged in bumpy accretions of tarnish and mold obscuring silver plating. A find to excite even the staunchest of atheists. Boxes of postcards from such places as Lourdes, the Pyrénées, Corsica, Paris, Nice, Menton, Tunisia, Algiers – Europa Exotica. The photos they contain are monochromatic, very dark, and their flipside contain cliché-ridden, vicissitudinal details written in a most elegant, feminine script not even then worth reading. Some of the postcards show scenes of the city when it was a rural, uncluttered, undeveloped metropole.

Armoires riddled with insect tunnels and stocked with decades of old clothes that, unfolded and held up to the torso, seem to have regenerated into style. Another spice tin full of old coinage. Coins minted of real silver but owing to governmental changes, they have been devalued into only a fraction of their worth. Mostly five, ten, and fifty franc pieces that look priceless. Drawers replete with skeleton keys that no longer open any-thing, not even the drawer they're in. They are striking in their burnished gold patinas, length and heft. Having kept one on my key chain, and transporting it to the States, others often ask me if it is "real".

Two very odd photographs of two children hamming it up and dressed as an angel and pitchfork-wielding devil. No one recognizes the children.

A series of photographs of a handsome Vietnamese man in military uniform standing next to what looks like his brother or close friend.

Behind a steel trap door that blocks where there once was an opening of a fire pit, yet another rusty cookie tin that when opened is alive with what was once someone's set of teeth. A ghastly thing to find. They are immaculately fringed in solid gold bridgework. The matron of the household congratulated me on this discovery. When I told her that these disembodied teeth may cause me nightmares she said, "That's silly, they can't bite you anymore."

Buried under bags of wool that was once used to stuff mattresses, a bronze statue of St. Louis sleeps. He is crowned and holds another in his outstretched hand, his other hand on the hilt of his sword. He wears a coat of mail, an armor vest emblazoned with a cross, and dons a magnificently large cape. Humidity has colored his eyes green.

Portraits, solemn and leering, of Jesus and Mary, in decorative wooden frames obliterated by hungry insects. The two have big round eyes that calculate my every move.

A wooden bust of an African beauty. On its underneath, she reveals herself to be of Madagascar descent.

Another tin container that contains recent money. With a little prying of the lid and of the matron, the money is revealed to be that of the baker's wife (the bakery is directly below). It is a mere forty francs that she will most likely never see again. She was hiding it from her husband.

The last item to be recovered from the past is a fifty-pound bag of coffee beans dating from the distant past. The beans are contained in a cloth potato sack and are of an exceptionally light, vanilla color and etched in black capillaries of their former essence. Most of the beans have been dotted by insect tunnels. The matron insists that they are still good. My only reply is that I would like to renege on my request of a traditional afternoon espresso.

The dust in the room is so chokingly thick and putrid that I blow traces of it from my nose for up to a week after the cleaning. At one point during the perusal, the billowing clouds of dust almost made me vomit. The asthmatic cough garnered by the exploration, or rather exorcism, remained for two days. It comes back by feint of memory anytime I enter the room.

By scrubbing the ancient tiled floor and re-stucco-ing its walls and putting up a fake ceiling of thin wood beams and panels, the room is once again made habitable. The refurbishing took nearly a month of hard labor. The matron agrees it is much more useful now and that she'll use it only to store herbs to be dried as she approaches with a tray of *apéritifs* and, trailing behind, bundles of thyme, rosemary, heath, and dill collected from local hillsides. Out of her housedress pocket spill albino coffee beans.

Rooms never
without views

Ladies who walk knowing that they're being watched, or wanting to be, not even caring the age or attractiveness of the onlooker. Women who dress not for the world, but themselves, elegantly.

Men who strut in a self-confident, almost pugnacious gait. The phrase for it is *rouler les mécaniques.* They measure each step knowing they have a point to prove and are completely justified in their convictions. Boisterous, brazen, they hold open doors for the opposite sex and for the elderly. They have irrefutable positions concerning the upcoming trends in weather.

Children who in restaurants behave impeccably well and who never ever bring gigantic plastic toys into the dining establishment. On the street they joke, they play, they sing dumb songs, and at any given moment might break into an impromptu game of soccer, thus claiming the street their playfield.

Tiny dogs that urinate and defecate at will and who have total control of the human at the other ends of their leashes. Old ladies who act as, as it were, bathroom valets for their pets, cleaning up after them, and in some not so rare cases, performing doggie hygiene with Kleenex.

People who fill street corners, especially those with bakeries, on Sunday mornings with the cheery din of gossip, neighborhood happenings and rumor, while they use baguettes as informal conversational aides emphasizing their brilliant points of observation with symphonic flourish.

Market owners, fish vendors, bar patrons, opening their businesses while whistling or singing who by sheer force of personality and belief in the relevance of their chosen professions encourage a devoted following.

Cicadas and frogs congregating in forgotten remnants of farmhouses that these outskirts once contained, now residences, murmuring a jeremiad of the days of old.

City workers who discuss intimate details of their wives' families' histories so that passersby might substantiate their vocal positions on the matter at hand and offer a nod of empathy.

Shopping carts stolen for the treasures of ten franc pieces they once held in confidence. Parked in abandonment.

Billboards, ever hanging, always featuring a beautiful man and woman engaged in anything other than hawking the product suggested for sale.

Young men and women hauling boxes of fresh fruits and vegetables sometimes offering a taste of one to be eaten whole on the spot as an enticement to the delicacies within their bamboo-lined stores.

Standing placard advertisements for a delectable array of ice cream and frozen treats that lie buried in tabletop freezers in Lotto stores or even Tabacs.

Sandwicheries that display real-life plates of food that will be freshly made not instantly, but within lengthy hunger-filled minutes, promising meat and lamb expertly grilled.

A clean trickle of water washing the history of the day into a wave of ripening sea.

ENTRIES IN AN
UNKNOWN HAND

un répertoire

11 août 199-

Weekend spent cutting grapevines at a country house in Pertuis. *Mouches* that took chunks of flesh off my legs, barely bearable heat, endless *vignes sauvages,* thorn bushes, weeds. The green grapes were incredibly sour, yet from time to time, I had to suck their bitter juice out of the need of pure thirst. It, with the sun anvil-ing on the back of my naked neck, makes for a painfully dizzy drunk that is one-half immediate hangover.

Rain has begun again, wiping out the heat. Bubbles slide across the red tiled-terrace. The sound of drops falling are in English. Addicted to the mother tongue, at night, sleeping on a terrace, a mattress bed enough, I surf the AM airwaves for radio programs from England, the Netherlands, Canada, Frankfurt, and occasionally Los Angeles. Some nights they come in loud and clear, even National Public Radio can be attained. But nothing is happening in America because, frankly, nothing ever does.

14 août 199-

People in the streets eye me with a modicum of suspicion and perhaps interest as I continue to deposit American mailbags of useless junk into their privately owned dumpsters. Dogs bark at me wherever I go. Morning light is uncharacteristically bright, sight itself can see too far, the scenery is empty with collines and trees and a swelling, tumescent sea. I toss and turn into a half-awake riddled sleep. What is the purpose of fear? The air from the sea is headstrong.

15 août mardi

Day of the Assumption. No money to buy cigarettes. Daily arrangement of Zen garden of sand within the terrace flower box: sea stone, eroded tile, tree sprouts, a Christ from a crucifix. Some clouds above the sea. Nothing for the day planned. Future is nothing unless it includes being together with a someone, then a world. Night waves are too strong to swim in. Underwater living, if it is without remembrance, is a possibility.

16 août mercredi

Mornings are most difficult. Men are working on the streets — beginning at 7:30 a.m. jackhammers begin. I have inhabited a room divided in two by a pipe, raised, beyond floor level. My only access to the outside world is shortwave radio. The reflection that greets me in the mirror: a stranger becoming more subtle in his disguises. *Peut-être* that age brings.

A seagull crosses the window. Time is in essence, endless work to be done.

17 août

Jackhammer and clouds. Dreams of a fractured self replete with moveable jaw section. So bright in the mornings that I exist like a troglodyte under a pillow and blanket until the heat compels me to rise. Must join the real world to buy croissants, milk, bread, essentials. Realize that I'm keeping a journal toward some kind of resolution. In France, there is nothing to be resolved.

20 août

The night ends with too much wine. Had to pee so bad that I used a rainwater bucket and oh my gosh the noise it made (too afraid to use bathrooms not my own). Discovered a wonderful park nearby: 19th-century buildings, palm and bamboo trees (in Europe!), ponds, cypresses, French bunker houses, bicycles from ages past, Monet bridges and catalpa trees made for lounging in. I count on the hours I'll spend there, in the mornings, alone. No letters arrived today and unfortunately tomorrow is Sunday.

21 or 22 août

Functioning here is a problematic magnified. In the face of history and custom. An outsider. Unable to function at the basic level: to make a call; I cannot understand, though I hear, what people say to me. A hearing deaf mute. Will not eat today, something decided. Water is enough. The radio and maybe even sleep.

23 août

Les marteaux-piquers awake me again. Last night it rained like it rains in the Midwest. Lightning close and fantastic. I have been called for jury duty in Utah. Have resolved to resolve nothing.

24 août

Someone calls and informs me that they have had an affair and it resulted in an already aborted pregnancy. Another friend lost a daughter to paralyzation due to a motorcycle mishap and I wonder if these things occur here, but at a much slower rate. Then I selfishly wonder if I have died and have been trapped in a joint French-Italian B-movie production.

25 août

The petit mistral has arrived to dust the city. In the morning, a trip to Samöens, what my limited mind envisions as the Rockies (only much better). It will be my second, after an airplane perspective, view of the Alps. This time it'll be my turn to see if the passes rise unexpectedly and if the peaks aspire theatrically. Wordsworth in the New Age music of the Romantics.

27 août

In the Hautes Alpes. Much more beautiful than anywhere in the American West. Mountains have definite knife blade shapes as if they are sculpted to be sharp. Villages are not so touristic and are worth stopping in because they are as medieval as the fountains they contain. Above them in the distance limpidly hang paragliders. It's only fitting that Mont Blanc is obscured by clouds. Swiss chalets surround. The people are real and generous – we stay in a resort hotel (off season) for free! The air is cool and the scenery is movie-like for an American. Unfortunately, hiking is out of the question due to time constraints. A moving tour of paradise from a car window.

8 août

In Val d'Isère. The Alfa Romeo we were driving broke down. This morning, IT IS SNOWING. The surrounding mountains, for they are rumored to be there, are invisible in winter clouds. August. The hotel's television features news in British.

29 août

Off a motor route, we stop for a picnic and I make a small fire because we are at six thousand feet or higher and it is cold. Almost immediately, men from the forest service discover us and make sure our fire isn't too big. They wear kepis and are very cordial. We offer them glasses of wine and French bread sandwiches of *saucisson.* They decline and tell us to be careful. This is civilization. Under pine trees, mushrooms bloom.

2 septembre
Essence might very well be cigarette smoke.

4 septembre

The date is becoming harder to calculate. Have returned to Marseille. Sleep becomes difficult to leave. Went hiking. Here the air is semi-tropical. There are palms and gently swaying pines. My sister sends me a green tomato from her garden in southern California. I will patiently wait until it reddens.

8 septembre

Or perhaps it's the seventh. No longer convinced of the relevance of time. Spoke to E. Ronsard at the Poetry Centre at the Vieille Charité while we smoked together. Thrilled to discover that Jerome Rothenburg will read in October. Outside, in the streets, an ambulance passes with its bleating of "Errrr-Errr."

11 septembre

A blanket of clouds over the city and its sea. Discovered the Pastré – an old 19th-century château that is now a museum for porcelain works. If the museum is of little interest, it has plantation-like grounds that are unword-able. Acres of Aleppo pines and white rock hills, an uncovered canal that seeps through its acreage like a lost river, adjunct building in the form of an Italian mountain getaway. Today, underneath my window, a man went through the garbage can, making an inventory of the stuff I've thrown away. He laughed at the old plates, *jouets*, clothes I released from non-memory. And he didn't take a thing.

15 septembre

I venture out to a free dental clinic where I am to have my teeth checked. Among the Arabs and Africans who speak French much better than I, there is a large contingent of homeless Poles, in need of care desperately. No one spoke much English. Afterwards, I take an intellectual trip to Les Arcenaux — what used to be a weapons storage facility on the water. It is now, drained ages ago, a very high-class part of the downtown, just off the port. The building contains apartments for artists on its highest floors, and underneath a large bookstore/expensive restaurant where the brightest and most moneyed dine. Pots of burgeoning plants line its cavernous entryway. I am at least three worlds away from the riches it contains.

17 septembre

Across the street from where I am living is a tiny atelier. It is called L'Estaminet, the definition of an artsy pub. Plans to go there and view the anonymous art it has to offer. The day promises to be cloudy but is not. Such changes in the weather can only be gauged in real time. Restaurants and bars packed at one a.m. The city is constantly packed with alive, living people. Bought some candy from a beachside vendor who I am sure weighed a part of his fat thumb in the transaction. The candy, mostly licorice, is exquisite.

18 septembre

It's memories that cease to stop. I recall friends from childhood in a leafy river town, that I would have never recalled until coming here. Europe is confusion and beauty and more of both. Leafy green and vines. The pond I ran away to once. Strangest thing of all, is that it is here. Manifold. Manifest.

21 septembre

The air here is as cool as a clean eating utensil. They are printing in the newspaper a lunatic's manifesto in the States. I miss out on such freak shows. The mail threatens bills. I write letters to friends who never write back. The present tense is that: tense.

25 septembre

Mountain air. Sanity guaranteed: books *en anglais* at the public library. To converse again with Poe, Hawthorne, Melville, others many others is a relief. The loose tiles in the bedroom sound like a strike in bowling when walked upon. A modern art museum and park three blocks away. Today will be a day of collecting plants from the hills. They are such foreign, flowering calligraphies of green.

30 septembre

Despair due to erroneous job leads, *boulots* that sound good but pay nothing. Uncertain plans like when to go to Paris and not ever wanting to return there. Freedom of not having any money. Another sunny day daring happiness. A walk in the hills after another last cigarette.

3 octobre

A lonely day with only housework to do. The sea is magnificent, a *mer agitée,* sharp hills of waves, a solitary island swum to be visited by seagulls and no one else, except the dried body of a goat, disappearing crabs just when the eye finds them, straight white eroded nubs of cliffs surrounded by the very definition of blueness. Islands barren of all meaning.

6 octobre

Endless travail. Mopping, scrubbing, painting, lifting, moving, taking many breaks. Continuing the cleansing of an abandoned wing of the house. Thousands of plates (real china), saucers, one dead mouse, six soup tureens. Will paint the steps leading up from the entrance the shade of Matisse's Red Studio and the blood of this will never leave my fingertips. Rained like rain will rain and I have thus been cordially introduced to the roof's many leaks. Buckets everywhere.

8 octobre

Today it is London outside. A thick fog purges the city of its scenery and vividness. It enters the room and obscures the windows. It makes seagulls weep with pleasure.

14, 15 octobre

A slight drizzle in Pertuis. The Luberon rises over cloud, a margin indicating place or indicating indication. Appropriate raindrop hits fresh ink on the page. Friday and Saturday were grape picking days: four and one half tons. A sensual affair, sweet stickiness, a lot of sweat. Daddylonglegs live in the vines keeping ladybugs as their companions. Met Lolo the Provençal farmer whose skin was the color of earth. Washed, it would look the same. Two dogs, Beaucerons, slept near us, protecting us from wolves. Clouds kept it cool on Friday; burning October sun on Saturday. Hauled buckets of grapes, two at a time, forty pounds each uphill to a tractor's cart, through sandy, sinking soil. Extreme aerobics. Saturday afternoon a glad escape back to Marseille to hear R. read and meet Roubaud of OULIPO fame. Driving back the sky was lit with pink neon fog. Walking through the Pertuis *paysage,* thyme grows to knee level, wild flowers bloom, grapes are bursting on the vine due to sexy ripeness. Sometimes the dogs get so thirsty they eat them. Birds do too.

18 octobre

The day is haze. Walking to the post office, where a game is played. The game goes like this: you give the attractive woman behind the glass (bulletproof?) your letters. She weighs and stamps them. Then, from her seat, fathoms behind the inch-thick barrier of glass, she says a number. You, who can't do math in your native tongue, must guess this number and replicate the guess in coinage. Sometime you even get it right. To celebrate, on the way home, buy bread.

20 octobre

When you don't understand much of what is being said around you, the television babbles in a tongue of Babylon, voices on the radio are more like music than the music is, the brain, not having to filter out distractions, has much time to exercise this newfound freedom. It obsesses, dreams up fantastic scenarios, takes the subconscious on adventures never ventured, turns to mortal thoughts. The frog who was residing on the terrace is gone, or has no comment.

22 octobre

Went swimming after a hike through the hills (mountains in my heart and lungs' interpretation) of many miles. The rocks are blooming purple with heather and October has so far only yellowed the sumacs. Half fell, descended a cliff that afterwards on my hiking map should only be attempted with ropes. Here, in overcrowded Europe, the *calanques* south of Marseille to Cassis, a protected area, it is pure rugged nature ranging from desert-like rockscape, to bowers and forests of pine trees. There are no people at all. Found myself in a stretch, a tree-lined balcony of tall pines call the Wood of the Valkyries. Underneath the overhang is a rocky inlet that features a cave and what the map reveals to be a cistern. Over the hills is a water purification plant, so the water may be indeed polluted, and if it is so, then it is sacrilege. The sense one has being here, in this remote place, is utterly sacred, dream-like, a cliché of what a tropical paradise might be. Swam anyway, for the briefest of moments to cool down. There are only birds here and views of islands.

3 novembre

A cockroach crawled out of my sleeve onto my bare hand as I was having breakfast today. And I didn't even flinch. The mistral visits and has been here for two days. It freezes the unsuspecting to the bone and throws up clouds of dust. There is nothing one can do within its midst except 1) talk about it and 2) complain.

9 novembre

Promise tomorrow of a voyage to the Var, then Mt. Peyroux in the southwest. The sun is constant sometimes brewing up a soup of clouds. The weather is cooling and this must be some type of sign.

21 novembre

Down to calling ads in the paper for a job. A possibility for a theatrical production: met an English woman, who knows an Irish man, and he knows of an Australian trapeze artist, and this might lead to a creative something. None of us speaks the same language. I have taken to walking the city much. On top of learning the language, I'm learning body language because in Marseille, gestures speak louder than words. Tonight's projects: cut my own hair and superglue my shoes back into walking order.

2 décembre

Drive to Mt. Peyroux in bad weather: low-slung clouds and bouts of rain. The countryside to me looks like Oklahoma because I can only see a quarter mile in any direction. Stay in a friend's magnificent, in the process of renovation, row house that has a ground level room for receiving visitors (including a piano and fireplace); a second floor that contains the kitchen and bathroom and a study; a third level whose ceiling is wood-beamed and offers a hallway with two sleeping chambers on either side. I have never entered a structure so small, complex, interesting, homey.

We visit a friend of a friend who is an art director for movies in England. Her house is even more medieval and more in need of (ongoing) restoration. She is incredibly beautiful, all the while knowing it, and tells us a story of how her wealthy family back home put her furniture on lorries aimed in this general direction. Apparently, in one of her dressers, French officials found a questionable substance and confiscated both the substance and the article of furniture, but did not turn her in. She tells us that the confiscatable material is probably owned by the man she hired to move her stuff, and she is very gracious that the French innately understood this, thus freeing her from a sticky situation. While she tells us this tale, she must go upstairs and press — vocally and mentally — the men she hired to re-do her sleeping chambers according to her English schedule. Her place looks like either a magazine feature, or a period piece (early twentieth century) from a movie in production.

A dog wanders into the kitchen and poops in it. The English woman holds her head in her hands and rubs her temple. Our laughter ends up making her laugh.

After more glasses of wine than we should have had, we return to our friend's home. We make an appetizer of *tapenade* and settle into the drizzly evening. We drink more and play songs on her stereo. We talk of America and how wonderful it seems so far from it. After our meal of ground olives, garlic, and anchovies, with bread and incredible cheeses, we retire to our room. On the wall is a painting, covered by a bed sheet, of a nude woman. Her hair, like our friend's, is red. We ask no questions and sleep to the accompanying rain.

10 décembre

No mail for a week. No buses for days; yet another strike. Meeting with the dream theatre group and reading Shakespeare out loud, which must count for something. Walking the streets of Mazargues for there is nothing else to do or needs to be done. To live. To experience where you are. The lesson France has taught me.

Hiking the hills that are as green as summer. Perfect weather. Birds circle the downtown and rain the streets with shit. After exercising, one needs only to return to a shower, then catch a bus downtown to live the city life. A city rimmed by nature is existence made whole. Not to forget the always interesting painting that aligns the distance: the sea.

17 janvier

Eating store-bought cookies in the hills above the city and they taste like the golden apples of the moon.

18 janvier

Must admit that my bathroom of choice is the one behind the foot of the stairs. The sink supplies cold water only and the toilet is chain pull. There is no room in it for a northern European to move about in comfort. Yet in this tiny chamber, I find the utmost peace: listening to the voices of people in the bakery and the grocery store on the other side. To live privately, among others, like an unintentional voyeur, heightens the senses. I shave, wash my body, brush my teeth, in a wailing stream of ice.

19 janvier

The hills are seductive. I march towards them only to be turned back by rain. Nothing to write.

17 février

Life and its various happenings – too much to record. Cold wind blowing, sunny skies. 11-13C. Letters from the U.S. are becoming quite rare. My friends have forgotten who I am (was).

25 février

Found myself on the banks of the Rhône today. Arles. Comforting to see the familiarity of a large river. Repulsive too: same stink all rivers have, same monotony of the flow, the dull continuity of life made into water. Lion-headed bridge half disappeared. Tomorrow it's to the Alps. Will try to go skiing in the mountains, if my knees will allow it. It will be such a different place that, already, I want to steal things from it.

28 février

Tonight, my nephew, who is visiting, says to me after I pull some feathers from his pillow, "Is there a bird in it." He has never before experienced the concept of down.

24 avril

Ventured to Roussillon and absconded from there with bags of deeply red, fine sand. Finally crossed the Luberon by car. Have hiked maniacally through these white hills bordering Marseille. Once I reached the sea on a hellish track of pure tallus, all downward, not thinking of the journey back. Once I got to its edge, ate a lunch of bread, cheese, saucisson and cursed the burning Mediterranean sun. The afternoon was hallucinatory in its clarity.

From the plateau of the deadman, I saw the city of La Ciotat, the mountain of Ste. Baume, and Ste. Victoire. These are visions meant for much greater persons than me.

Returning to the city in the same day, I go to the library and find books on Joseph Cornell, most of Kerouac's better works, even John Fante! I could live like this forever. Each day is an unsuspected gift.

The unknown sea plants I am cultivating on the terrace are blooming purple and yellow flowers. Have never been the parent to such beauty before.

29 avril

All today, rain and clouds that tore themselves to barely expose the tops of the hills. Some hung like UFOs above the city and the nearest beach. A steady drizzle not even enough to make an umbrella worth carrying yet it brings out the colors and true smells of springlife. Flowers and trees and a solitary birch in the wetness and lights of an abandoned Parc Borély bore an ecstatic vision just moments before the night patrolman kicked me out.

2 mai

Clouds tear through the hills Japan-like. Sun occasionally illuminates the city and its humdrum of fog. Much mailing to be done. I'm in a fever of stasis. The doors here seem too heavy to ever dance with or hug.

19 mai

How the specificity of dates account for nothing. Days as constant ebb. For three miserable days, clouds capped the tops of the hills in a stole of cobweb. These clouds sometimes change direction and float in, landward. The weather is warming and one can swim in the still a-little-too-cold water. Wildflowers, everywhere, fields of blood red poppies, activated and singing!

16 17 18 mai

Had an incident in which I nearly came to blows with the bakers who work below. The fact of the matter (to use such a phrase) is that they owe the family above years and years of back rent. Defended the family I live with. Three anonymous men of Marseille origin attacked me verbally, harshly. I cussed them out in bad French. Playing the role of husband, father man. The only pleasure from the incident came with this afterthought: what little some people have in life to become passionate about. For the first time in my life, I acted Latin.

25 mai

Days here are art. I find a tabernacle at a second hand store. The local museum is showing Russ Meyer flicks. There is an ancient, paint-stripped picture frame awaiting pick-up by the garbagemen that I intercept.

7 juin

These days pass like salt in urine. So many things have occurred: Céline's funeral, letters arrive, finally, from friends, summer arrives in a day. Just like that. Stomach sickness: I ate severely fresh lamb chops at a nice restaurant and my body couldn't handle it. Here, the voices of the living filter through the windows in the morning better than any chiming of an alarm clock and I wonder when I will be able to truly join them.

22 juin

The unspeakable ambiguity that engulfs me. Have visited Toulouse where I walked that sad medieval city's bridges and quays. Some French Arabs ask me if I have a cigarette, to get my attention. They want to sell me hashish. It is a city so much influenced by American culture that it's spooky.

Back in Marseille, days are spent underwater with marine life, my truest of friends. In the afternoons, I collect plants and firewood from the hills. The city is bursting in music and the temptation of nightlife. They are throwing a series of *fêtes* solely for the reason to celebrate life and have fun.

24 juin

Strangely cold day due to the wind. Lightning and thunderstorm, booming, like in the American Midwest. Begin a project of peeling horrendous wallpaper, patterns straight from Kubrick's *A Clockwork Orange*, from walls in a room. The walls underneath are bright yellow. Letters to friends are written and perhaps there will be a trip to Dijon to see a writer who has befriended my strange existence here.

8 juillet

Summer downpour. Oddly cool temperatures. Strange cloud-shows with no applause. Hiking the *calanques*, resting under umbrellas of pine. Reading much, things I would have never read – Hawthorne, Melville, Emerson. So desperate to connect with English it's a process much akin to viewing pornography. Not real, but satisfying. Snow is reported in the Alps and the Pyrénées. Nips of winter in the air that bite at the neck and shoulders. Nature's attempt at foreplay.

12 juillet

Overwhelming joy – fixed the chain pull toilet so that it doesn't drizzle on its occupant. Life made tons more bearable by such a minuscule victory.

13 juillet

Blue mountains, turning purple. Pizza on the beach. Rare grooves such as this . . .

27 juillet

Day after my birthday. Slight rain today – in America there's an Olympic bombing and an unfathomable plane crash. In France, life proceeds as it always has. Terrible humidity, though, so I sleep on the roof terrace in a tent. Isn't life swell/swelling?

PILGRIMAGE

A raid of pigeons tapping at the windows. Stones are thrown to scare them away. Pillar of bread, pillar of cement, pillar of pepper, pillar of pillars rotting to sand.

Fountain in the park endlessly, until winter, flowing. Children ride new bikes, looking for new friends, new toys, trails, new birds and brush animals, stopping to talk to different parents.

In the depth of night, movement is heard in the kitchen, a tinkering. Washed dishes, silverware, a dunce hat *quignon* of bread, bugs inventorying old discoveries.

Cherries, unpicked, fall to the ground and split open with ripeness. Dogs come down with colic. Under the tree, a pig farm of living ruins.

The bus waits for us. At the post office, the worker is sympathetic, offers a choice of overseas stamps. No line at the bakery. On her perch, the golden lady casts her lot of daily, mute miracles.

Throughout the night, a machine hums, creates a stream of foam in the street. Dogs don't sleep, cats are agitated. Across the *poissonnerie,* bones of mermaids wash by.

On the roof: inevitable black cat wearing a white tie. Motionless, it waits for birds and butterflies hungry not for food, but a murder.

Mingled on the street with everything else, a water-soaked baguette, clothespins, empty box of cigarettes, fallen fruit, a braid of haircut at the barber's.

CHEMIN DE LA FEMME MORTE

These hills that are by-lines meandering through the past, stop in the present. Haze apparent, the day, without gloom, a see-through.

Wind again, searches the alley in complete disregard to the hazard it makes. Cats disappear. Windows break. Birds disdain the sky. Babies can't breathe. All hats off to November's calling card, blown away.

A finite row of plowed sugar, the sea in wind. It is speculated that there are cave paintings in it, under it. It is speculated there is snow in heaven.

Small house abandoned, the corner of the street walled with stone, broken glass, futile barbed wire stretched into shapes of prospectors looking for treasure, a dressmaker's dummy.

Linseed oil painted on tile and left to capture footprints, leaves, flowers bloomed and spilt, feathers of magpies, ashes, the jewel of a false tooth.

A certain hour, daily, co-mingling scents of dinner. Music and clattering of dishes, tonight a feast. Signs remind us that government offices are closed for days. Early Monday morning, they'll get back to planning holidays.

Coldness descends and sticks to streets like litter, mostly un-wrappings. Men smoke more, women walk faster wearing black leather, returning to their second skins.

The story goes: she went to Toulouse to meet some friends. Story goes: she never came back. With so many pictures of her, on buildings, the news, the time is filled looking, missing. Lost.

Shots of hunters resound in the empty wildness. Hills, these cliffs that breach into villages, sometimes cities crowned with castle or church and enveloped in lavender and lumps of unseen poison.

Because space must be conserved, families are buried on top of each other, each person a level of history. On the tomb are plaques that read: *in memory, without you, souvenir.*

It's a querulous affair: when to return the ladder. In between appointments with the doctor, daily visits to the fruit stand, expected unexpected callings from neighbors, the day passes as if there were really something to be done.

In youth, she posed as a nun. How many, many photos wearing a wooden cross, hands clasped in sincerity, lips pressed together, ironed white habit, hair concealed as cloth.

Her husband fell while climbing a mountain; she keeps pictures of him on the walls, has sold or given away his possessions. She takes meals on the terrace, with a view of the low Alps, where he is now somewhere beyond. Across from her, an empty plate.

A minimum of labor is done, but accomplished her way. She waits for just the right time to hand over a bag of cookies, small cakes, a bottle of lotion, and a rabbit's head for the dog.

She is old now but her hands are still young, being a seamstress in her spare time. She asks a customer to try on the skirt, we are both busy with work, separated by a sudden nudity.

He picks apples in Italy, when in season, working every other day, the year was bad. From Hungary, he waits in doorways, collecting money he'll share, half and half, with the whores.

No bones about it: lunch hour, streets are alive with hunger. In front of the sandwich shop a line of impatient speculators; wooden crates bloodied with hooves.

Her façade, the oldest in the village, something of which she is proud. On Sunday evenings, at the piano practicing music and mastering being alone.

There's not much to say, so they yell. Body language is *commedia dell'arte.* The cars suffer minor scratches in an accident. The people, for the given moment, act as who they are: lovers savoring random passion.

In the bar there's always more smoke than inspiration. So the waitress bends at the waist to replace a napkin on the table, noticing her body every inch as much as you do.

Incremental. Four fish for dinner. At the hospital where Rimbaud died, the plaque is mostly unread. And in photography books of nudes, the pictures are there, never torn out, defiled, stolen.

That her breasts are blooming with a fungus of nervousness referred to as mushrooms, she walks the rain-dampened hills and a trail studded with so many reminders.

Holidays of another country pass by, here we celebrate the return of winter birds. *Mésange* on the doorstep, seeking the Gnostic origin of crumbs.

End of the district: a church and bus stop. There are the regulars, men in hats, kids going to school, pigeons waiting for a ride, and Christ just hanging around.

One large, not too bad, nude hangs on the wall, covered in haste by an old textile, creases can be seen in both. We are guests of another sort.

Avenue du point d'interrogatioN

Rather do nothing. Than have nothing to do. Finally, no rain lasting for days. Kids from Catholic school light up outside the walls, hurrying to be adults. Scooters zooming towards afternoons of television, parents at work, and sex.

Claiming the black under her fingernails is blood from the hearts of artichokes, she continues with dinner, then the dishes, with dirty hands that will never come clean.

Summit is stumbled upon as a crown, a cross, a fallen cross. Hills are white with envy: they will never die.

What is not usual is merely coincidence. Those who don't gamble appear when there are stakes, toting umbrellas. Glory is as thick as coats of white paint on windowsills. Gathering around kiosks to hear the papers speak of a stolen plane that flew through the legs of the Eiffel Tower again.

That mimosas are in bloom, it may be spring. Turquoise, blue waves, or anemones. Winter has left the beach, leaving behind its bra, and one leather shoe.

Hours of the park when no one visits. These noons of strays: cats, dogs, people. Koi of no particular gender.

Pillows on a makeshift bed, vegetable crates and wool stuffed mattress. Hastily sewn together, in canvass, they molt. With each sleeping, feathers.

Seeming to never rain again, fish merchants proudly display their stock. Blue crabs and white mussels, ropes salted by the sea. Reality almost ready to eat.

On the sides of roads they present themselves as weeds, these flowers of early March: never so many dandelions, forget-me-nots, strange red ones sung *coquelicots.*

In any given instance, an argument. About mail, unpaid water bills, the left open-ness of a door. So much civilization built into walls, and rain soaking history in mud.

Whether or not the bus will come is not known. Time shared tapping watches, wondering about shapes of feet fitted in shoes.

Lovers here offer no exception, they hairpin the beach and lawn its borders. In the park they lie in open theaters of their, and our, desire.

Wild irises in yellow and purple, acacia around the aqueduct as if it were Hiram's grave. Laughter in the chalk hills, of gulls; flesh the color of sand. Spring.

From afar, women in tight black pants at the beach, really only girls. Boys run in packs, shouting loud as the colors of their shorts, already men. The promise of sex, better broken.

Enjoying cigarettes in the sun, seasoned women in the almost nude. Threes of slow-burning aureoles.

In a pot on the roof long forgotten bloom weeds and their flowers: *soucis, pensées.* Better to leave worries and thoughts, alone.

Because it stormed so much we collected it in buckets and were reminded by a plastic bottle labeled *rain.*

Anxious people leave doors to get what's necessary: lilies on the first of May, sticks of bread protected by bats on handles, broken umbrellas they hold crucified.

In a jar, no – a glass – made for drinking she has kept cuttings of her finger and toe nails for these past thirty years. To prove, perhaps, or measure, how she has grown.

The first of May when everyone, it seems, is seen with freshly bought lilies-of-the-valley. When the hillsides bloom in downpours of flowers.

Warm day in winter distinguishable by traffic and the number of pedestrians and a flock of sparrows dotting the sky perceptible.

Where there were birds, now buildings. And the heels of uneaten bread. Out the window, billboards and other signs of attempted comprehension. Drapes patterned with a table and flowerpot. Ancient or modern, streets go one way: back.

Rug pattern woven with hair. Footprints of insects in the flour. Value of old stamps or money hidden in the linen. If feelings could be saved in a box, we, most assuredly, would hide it under the stairs.

Sea's only rival: clouds on a perfect day. Mountain's only friends are rocks; trees grow in them. We walk a path marked by red swaths of blood, or paint, to find nothing and the teepee of bones it left behind.

With trains, books, enemies, the mail, dirty dishes, and the next meal, grass, soap, dead birds, check stubs, promises on windy days, clouds and handkerchiefs, paperwork and bottles of wine, there's always more.

Time in between rains, a melon wrapped in foil. We walk from one antique dealer to another with a box of dusty crucifixes to sell. Why buildings without inhabitants crumble. Nothing to hold them down.

The lonely dog barks at sounds, all night. Throw it a piece of bread, for silence. In the chapel, there's a fresco portraying miraculous snow. The priest's breath smells of parchment. He shakes our hands, twice.

Wind visits by slamming a window. In so many days, not much to occur. We varnish the table, a hope for rain. The bakery is closed which is something everyone knows. Monday morning, urgently leashed dogs leave hoodoos of shit on the street.

Day begins in eternity, burnt bread and an audience of sparrows. Returning in September. A will is modified to include the newborn. So many keys to unlocked doors. Laundry hangs, in attendance, waiting to be worn.

Sun pools on the tiles. Potted plants stretch their roots. Beware of dog sign is now in use. Promenade of traffic has stalled, going somewhere. The bar opens. Only customers – bees.

An annex containing histories of shoes and purses no longer walked. Brilliant autumn light on skin. Regrets of flowers, having bloomed. Bread baked to be torn apart. At the bistro, waiters wait under sycamores, women talk of their new, blonde hair.

So many snail shells in the sand suggest a desert, the graveyard it hides. Rocks grow into trees, the light echoes; a valency, whatever it might be, happens. At the pass, painted graffiti, expected to be primal and in another language.

Seagulls, really mutes, try to talk while what we hear is begging. The park is cluttered with people and the flags of plastic they leave. If the word for sin is peach tree, there is no redemption.

Posters re-postered. New music comes, is played, goes. Children, locked in school, wait to erupt in energy that running cures. The bus empties itself at urinals of stops. Dogs parade home, attending corners, selecting trees and alleys, knowing exactly where they are going.

Old things are painted white, the simplest color of resurrection. The view from the *pissoire* is nearly the same picture every day, a study of realism. Boredom hits the big city in waves, nothing to do but kill.

Whatever the weather, pages in time layers, there's what's seen from l'Estaque. Any book or geographic dictionary in the crudeness of a public library: cold magazines, maps of an east, books used. Grocery lists better left unread. Great places to go: where you already are, just without the same, swaying, trees.

Old photos in another language, the people look vaguely the same. Separated at birth, families cling to umbilical cords of memory, powdered thought collects in luggage stored in rooms. Nothing is kept safe.

The rest being simplification, a pruning of the *citronnier* branches, crusts from bread left for pigeons, thread and needle unattached. Men in the street smile to each other. Coins, sad faces of, making music in their pockets.

A painted stairway, first step to the last, going up. Resulting in footprints or not anywhere to go. Rains came leaving calling cards of leaves. Snails try to enter an empty fishbowl.

Clover grows in the abandoned pot. The baker creases his dough with a screwdriver. Best secrets aren't ones kept. They're the ones everyone knows.

What pigeons do at night, still a mystery. On the roof, there's a pile of thread and key chains. View of the ocean is the same: blue plains. A puddle of sky with waves.

Bird of unknown origin. Castles were built so we could walk their ruins. In the mysterious hills, grapes are free. Surprised by an accumulation of stones, we find a cemetery for two, the plot of every happy story.

Though coins are few, they weigh more than they can buy. Though coins are few, they ring pleasant in the hand. Few are the coins, for buying time. Though coins are few, they are worth their fleeting weight, not in paper, only gold.

October at the beach and they are still swimming. To parachute, one must first practice. Ladies expose their backs to us, their breasts to the sun. A haze envelops the city we don't want to see anyway.

She keeps with her countless souvenirs of Lourdes, medallions, candles, coffee cups, playing cards, stacks of old, empty shoe boxes. Not knowing she will die one day and that these are, waiting in the wings, coffins.

When the garbage trucks come, no praise is offered, no one waves goodbye, nothing is missed, the men are anonymous in their soiled jumpsuits. We part with the things we once loved. The noise is expected.

News is a flower that has bloomed. In the port, boats embark to distant islands, other ports. Bells ring and bells ring unanswered. The metro smells like a sea underground. Police wait for bombs to never explode.

Fake coins for months are passed and used. Until the word gets out and nowhere will accept. A bum says if they're not real, then sell me imaginary cigarettes.

Wine for sale cheaper than bottled water. Dogs driven wild by scents wait outside the grocery store. Petted by an array of hands, they relinquish themselves to the leash of old leather, familiarity.

Hills are rending clouds again, there's nothing better for the weather to do. *Arbousier* blooms spiked red candies of fruit, free for the taking. In the city, the cemetery is empty with visitors. Opened, behind steel curtains, storefronts. Windows, baked goods, magazines, people. Saracens of the night in hiding. Each building, a castle remembered.

Arguments on the streets occur inevitably beneath windows drawn with sleep. Fewer sirens than horns. Trees in the park already have begun their silent march.

Lonely man who lives downstairs waits on the corner wearing ironed slacks. It's Friday night. His hair is parted in hopes it won't remain so.

Sea has made just claim to the view and filled the city with its margin. Notes are scribbled and abandoned. She was once a model, we remember as she sees us, trying to conceal groceries, pulled by a cart, with her still thin body.

The ladder must be returned to Elise who will say a few words to gain some in return. We both pretend to understand. The room fills with the purple smell and sight of a tarte borne from the oven.

Vegetable stand swarms with those expecting guests. Vendors brag about flavors of produce from Spain. A child eats grapes straight from the crate, everyone tries their hardest not to notice. Songs, old songs, from an old country, say Sardinia, played and sung over the airwaves. Grandparents around a t.v. set. A most harmless kind of death, nostalgia is.

If he looks like what he is, a certain time-honored nationality, Corsican or Dutch, he's said to have that type of head. Streets fill with the anonymity of *pieds-noirs*.

CAFÉ LIFE

It exists everyday, which is only logical, for it is what all life is based on. In some small establishments, plates of spaghetti are still served, or any sandwich dreamt of will be prepared if your face is agreeable enough to accompany such a request. Often what will be served are leftovers the owners didn't finish the night before, tasting just as good to the newcomer to the table.

There are large multi-level cafés that serve just about anything desired, including outrageous ice cream desserts or rich pies, tartes, cakes. These, though, are often very pricey and visited by professional shoppers and other snootier members of society.

Small cafés, what an American might call holes-in-the-wall, are the best. Their decor is dated, sometimes to the Fourth Republic. They always have white tile floors that haven't been washed since the last storm. Ricard or Cinzano sponsored advertisements, which make stealing an ashtray a necessity, cover the walls, outdoor umbrellas, and adorn shot glasses or glasses of *pression.*

Some of these café/bars have wooden wet bars. All are lined with interior mirrors and large windows that peer onto the street and racing world that whisks by, disinterested and hurried. Most of these places feature a battered cassette player or radio playing the radio. If not then the music of traffic, of the city being a city, permeates the walls. Plus intermittent whooshes of toilets being flushed.

Often the bartendress is the owner's wife or daughter and no matter her age, she is singularly beautiful. Classical in that she'll listen to any story you might have the burning desire to tell. For every story you have to communicate, she'll counter with two of her own. They will be even more lovelorn than yours and a tad sadder but free of remorse. She'll tell them and shake off the memories they engender with a wave of her hand in the air like a butterfly taking its initial flight and a gorgeous smile. Maybe even a wink.

The stories told in these places are always the same: love gone bad, unrequited love, how life seemed to be much better, simpler, ideal. When she speaks to you she'll grab and hold your arm. She'll whisper things you don't understand in your ear. She'll make you feel like everything you have to tell each other really matters only to people like you two. In cafés like this one, life and living it are the only things that matter.

The espresso is incredibly strong and sobering, served with three cubes of sugar that will be administered incrementally, stirred into the mix with a tiny spoon that beckons your tongue to play with its silver cupped hand. The small espresso cup, one fourth the size of the American version, will have originated elsewhere and will be marked so. Ones from *Les Trois Mages* turn up everywhere. They add an extra-legal charm and remind us that by naming something, it does not automatically mean ownership. In naming, metamorphosis and travel are more likely.

Even though most cafés serve alcohol, they really aren't places to get drunk. There is no social scene expected to occur, no happy hour, other than the natural occurrence of small, private, local gatherings of souls that mostly accrue from visiting regulars.

If you're a regular at a café, you are one of its family members. You have the opportunity to learn more about the owners and their lives than you might have ever bargained for. They will accept you without discrimination, unless you can't pay your tab. The owners aren't really interested in making a buck. They're more involved in spending their business hours, a vital chunk of their lives, with those they consider familiars. They like to familiarize.

The café itself is a desperately lonely place. There are so many of them on any given street, street corners, back alleys, that they promise anonymity for the cost of a drink. There is always room, even when it's lunchtime and it is packed. There will be one table in the far back corner, near the kitchen or bathroom. During the non-lunch-rush hours of the day, the café is mostly empty. It is home away from home.

What the café functions as is a place for the individual to go to not be him- or herself. Or to be him- or herself intimately with others or better, alone. Needless to say, they are great places to write. They are great people-watching venues. No one will bother you. The parade of interesting/beautiful people who pass by their windows rarely even musters a glimpse inside – more often they do their hair or fix their make-up in the window's reflection. They are lonely souls who accompany your lonely soul with a catwalk of fascination.

Cafés in France, with their cheap offering of the speed of espresso or the controlled buzz of a few *pressions,* their temptation of a peeled hard-boiled egg, are addictive little spots where one can relax with one's own id and ego. The superego can be left at the door.

They are places deep within the bustling internal organs of the city where one can subtract oneself from it all while being in the heart of the beast. Where one can kick back and relax and take in the passing scenery and meaningless complexity of life. They are places where books can be read in a glance. They are where waiters will give you matches for free if you tell them how good-looking they are. They are sacred pagan chapels where one may meditate on what it means to be an individual in history's unending stream of uniqueness mutated.

KEEPSAKES

Days that go by so smoothly, so ingrained in the rituals of meal preparation and wine drinking; clouds practicing tai chi as they pass from sea through and over the city and the crinkled border of mountains behind it all. It's much easier to calculate what day it is by measuring the assumed time that has passed from one rainfall to the promise of another. A melon missing a quarter of itself, wrapped in foil on a wooden table.

There's nothing much to do anyway except walk from one local antique dealer to the next within the immediate maze of the neighborhood of streets tree-lined and made occasionally barren by stretches of mortar walls behind which are tightly built houses and secrets we will never know.

Once, I found a collection of old crucifixes in a cardboard box next to a dumpster. They were beautifully crafted: gilded silver Christs pinned to varnished wood crosses. Large ones, small ones. If not truly silver, then shiny metal that resisted rust.

Beauty is in the eye as I found, much to my amazement, that none of the dealers wanted them. They said that their condition is very good, but there no longer exists a market for such goods. They suggested that I donate them to the church. For blessings.

This is what I did. That is, I left them on the doorstep of the small chapel behind a pizzeria – a sad little place that serves more as the priest's house than a gathering place for worship. No one but the very old ever attends Mass. Behind the chapel is a tiny meditation garden with a statue of the Virgin. She is surrounded by more weeds than trees. She is a once wild animal who let out of her cage roams nowhere. And she has no visitors. Other than dandelions.

The day after I made my donation, I find the box of crucifixes, with a few of the larger ones missing, next to the dumpster near the chapel. They are in the same dusty cardboard box. On one of the box's flaps is written this word in black marker: *gratuit.*

Incidental

The aforementioned chapel is on Boulevard des Neiges. The interior sports a fresco featuring a scene vaguely biblical – an artistic rendering of a place very similar to the surrounding one, set back in the somewhat distant past, and unexpectedly covered in a blanket of snow.

Rumor has it that long ago there was a holy snow shower in a province of Italy from where the original priest originated. The storm was a wrath that either stopped an invading army of infidels, or was summoned up to relieve a drought.

Only rarely does it snow in Marseille.

EscargoT

When it rains, as it does quite often in mistral-empowered downpours, even though the arid hills surrounding the town seem to contradict such a fact, and even hide such a possibility as this: snails appear in droves. Snails are legion. Snails rule the ground of Provence.

They have a dark blue, or black, line on their shells that emphasizes their Zen-like spirals of existence. Empty shells can be collected to be made into jewelry or wall decorations. They look like tiny Chinese blue and white porcelain teapots.

The elderly still wander fields after rainstorms, or in the morning when the dew makes field grass thick with moisture and bug life. They are collected not for artistic reasons, but for snacks.

Snails are cooked in their shells in the oven covered with a paste of garlic, crushed parsley, perhaps some bread crumbs that all boils with their natural juices into a tangy sauce. Incidentally, the larger, hardier snails carrying grey-brown shells with the textures of a toe or fingernail are the ones for cooking. They bubble away in their one-time homes that, after cooking, become finger bowls from which humans may slurp them down.

What do they taste like? There is no equivalent in the American palate. They are chewy and surprise the tongue with a taste, not strong, even kind of subtle, and oddly glutinous in texture. Personally, I've never been tempted to eat them after trying them once. Not because they are bad-tasting, but due to their overall like-ability as tiny, harmless creatures.

What is so amazing about snails is that they roam and range everywhere possible and im—. They crawl up walls made of anything, you find them in your shoes on a humid day, they attempt to enter and explore goldfish bowls, they are a minor nuisance.

What is so characteristically French about the French is that instead of developing a product to eliminate the ubiquitous slug, they resolutely put them in their place on the food chain: appetizers on a Gallic menu.

INCIDENTAL

There is a billboard, or is it letters painted on a building already existing, that in giant blue letters asks for our redemption: JESUS PARDONNEZ NOUS NOS PECHES. The building is in north Marseille, adjacent to the autoroute, so anyone coming into town can't miss it.

The first time I saw the message it read: Forgive us our fishes or peaches, Jesus. In French, the word for sin, *péché*, is akin to the English, peach; a *pêcher* being a peach tree. Finally, religion that makes sense.

BOMBS

During Christmas season, the Islamic Front, operating out of the former colony of Algeria, has an insidious habit of placing bombs on the Paris metro. This act of cowardice in turn brings out the French military on patrols of city streets, government buildings, and the underground.

Men, dressed in fatigues, sport machine guns and mean-looking guard dogs and the major cities take on an air of fortification and wartime effort. Initially, it's a disconcerting sight to see such force out casually mingling with civilian life. Marseille itself has little threat of an explosion due to the large North African population integrated into its multi-cultural Europeanized society. Why would radicals send the message of the possibility of injuring their own (as if they were capable of higher logic)?

It's a sight one has to grow accustomed to, as the existence of a military presence wanes from shock to rationalized sense of security for the civilian. If there ever is a bomb threat in Marseille, it is of Corsican Separatist origin. It is an all too real theater of unrest and protest heir to Europe's turbulent past. For an American, it is a reminder that fear is an all too real drama that the populace must psychologically partake in.

Protest is a viable form of expression. Violence can occur whenever. This is the case even during localized strikes of the bus or city workers. When rallies are held, hell may just break loose. Groups of strikers form in front of Marseille's seat of government, the Préfecture. Loud music is played and banners are waved. The people shout and sing. The riot police, the infamous CRS, suit up in their black riot gear, with shields, batons, and tear gas grenades attached to their holsters. They look even more menacing than the enchanting young army men.

The CRS set up steel barricades that block pedestrian traffic, as pedestrians argue with them to let them through, just this once. The guards banter with the strikers. Each is just doing their job. Unless a drunk striker gets too rowdy and begins throwing stones or bottles, there won't be any action. Rarely does it come to blows. This is Europe's legacy of free speech embodied in its colorful, energetic demonstration. It is what Revolution has become today. A theater of re-enactment.

Radical political opinion is tolerated in this manner. One day, theater workers might be protesting their low wages and lack of job security. The next day it will be a rally to free Tibet from Chinese harassment. One wonders what might actually happen, and how it would occur, if these crowds actually stormed the Préfecture. Probably, all the officials would have already gone home for the day.

The fact that the right to express heartfelt opinions is taken seriously in this brilliantly staged public play enables those with convictions to participate in groups of individuality and give them and onlookers and the police a break from the routine of life. It is a process that has to be orchestrated in the U.S.

In the action of halting everyday monotonous life, life is enhanced while being postponed. A space to reflect upon life is created within a parenthesis of the passing hours of the day. The stoppage of the expected causes inquiry into the reasons why.

The populace, differing in opinion, background, heritage, political leanings, are united by this process of expression that toys with everyone's sense of the mundane. That is why in America, all Mondays are mundane.

WALKING THE LUBERON

It's always an uphill battle. There are slowly undulating fields of grapevine, there are downhill treks on which you must slalom across the path or gravel road to keep the legs from running. There are pools of trees and shade, thin streams of water, sunburnt outcrops of stone, and in the rocks that have fallen from those stones, pools of rainwater drying in cups of grey burnished sandstone.

The soil is rock-studded and chalky, but it can too be rich and moist, covered in fungi and moss carpets. The air in the Luberon smells crisp even on hot days when it burns the incense of distant forests of cedar. Variety is the source of its forested life.

The foothills contain mostly small farms that devote themselves to the production of wine grapes. They are far apart and each is well hidden from another by natural fences of woods and trees. The farm houses, or *mas,* may be decked with horses, a series of older cars that never ran all that well, perhaps even chickens, roosters, and pigs. Often walking the Luberon's trails private property is inadvertently crossed and one can take a peek at the hodgepodge collection of stuff farm life naturally assembles: no longer used for anything bathtubs, tractors and their parts, piles of half burnt wood, wheelbarrows with holes rusted through their once blue underbellies, invented (shoddily) beehive houses made of scrap wood, a compilation of useless things set outside (for eternity) among naturally occurring vegetation with cake slices of mountains diminishing in the distance seem to take on a greater meaning. What can humanity construct that has the relevance of a pastoral view?

If you happen to be out and walking on an overcast day and you find yourself among oak, maple, pines, past farms and isolated, abandoned-looking homes, over hilltops that mostly abscond their views by growing trees and scrub prodigiously, underneath on lower levels balconies of stone that might or might not give way to a clearing where the misty skies and crooked steps of farther off mountain ridges patiently await your arrival, you might just happen upon a couple of menhirs planted into the earth. Headstones. A private, secluded cemetery. To be buried here.

OCTOBER BEACHES

Back in Marseille, it's still possible to swim in the late reaches of October. The water, not being oceanic, stays warm, and like the temperature during a clear day, is most invitingly turgid at four in the afternoon. The Mediterranean, being a land-surrounded sea, warms up in strata in the spring. In March, the surface to about six inches deep contains the sunrays and is at least ten to fifteen degrees warmer than what lies below. By April, you can easily wade in – from your feet to your kneecaps it is freezing – but from the knees up it's a veritable soup.

When the water is warm enough to swim, surprisingly few beach-goers jump in. Even in the desperately hot summer months most people prefer to roast on the stony lip of this gigantic salty swimming pool. Those who do enter the water are of the extremes of age: the elderly and little children. Gorgeous young women bake away their youth into deep shades of bronze and brown on the shore. Men lie on the beach like pretzels requiring the compliment of mustard. Many choose to merely shower the heat away rather than submerging themselves in the cool belt of turquoise, then farther out, deep band of resplendent blue.

Probably, their biggest hang-up is the vast amount of spiky sea urchins peopling the rocks below the surface. There isn't any threat of sharks and very little pollution and trash at the better beaches. There isn't any imaginable reason to stay out of the

Mediterranean liquid jewel. Perhaps, to the veterans of fun, it's old news.

From an American perspective, it's a most inviting swimming pool, replete with dryads, whose banks would be burgeoning with people drinking beer and cooking hamburgers on hibachis. The Mediterranean is a source of sacrament, revitalization, relaxation, and pure joy that the French completely take for granted.

CANTONNIER

The *cantonnier's* presence is known by his calling cards: rags bundled in the streets. His job is to open the underground plumbing of the city (fire hydrants don't exist) so that the resulting surge of water, with his rags used as breakers, creates a stream of cleansing force that rivulets the gutters, sidewalks, streets, and curbs.

To control the flow in a primitive yet artistic swash of hydrology, his tool of choice are bundled rags tied into knots, thrown to the ground, that absorb and redirect the spring-like water's path.

The effect is one akin to a governed flood – a simultaneous eruption of mountain springs within a section of city streets. Interesting flows and drainage patterns are created by his rag placements. Since the work is serious business, children don't dare play, float sticks or leaves, in the mini-canyons of tiny grandeur. The day's garbage and stains are washed away in the controlled flushing. The sound of trickling water cools the ears with a meditative burbling. It is a most sacred way to maintain cleanliness in the city, these effervescent Zen fountains of the quotidian.

Homeless

The homeless aren't so homeless in France in the disconnected-from-everything reality the concept connotes in the U.S. Generally speaking, they seem to have more of a chance of finding a place to stay, or existing un-alone, in Europe. Sometimes there are friends, or friends of friends, or friends of friends of family, or there are hostels, houses of prostitution, and in the forgotten margins of the city abandoned buildings or hedges in parks that conceal living places between stone walls, or large wooded fields awaiting commercialization bordered by chainlink fences with inviting gaping holes. The police leave them be.

The temporarily destitute dress pretty well considering their lot in life: jeans, decent long-sleeved shirts, and they shower and shave at least once every few days. In a crowd, they are imperceptible. They announce their caste when they appear alone.

What they do, rather than panhandle, is to stand at the door of a post office (in France, *La Poste* is also the bank for many) and they open the door for customers. In their hands they hold a small saucer in which the generous may place a few coins. They do not ask for money. They simply greet you with a "Bonjour." They attempt to incorporate themselves into the greater society that has somehow rejected them by providing a favor for one in return. Spare change.

Many today hail from Eastern Europe, in search of the French version of the American dream (it comes with more beautiful women and better food). Socialism gives them the benefit of rudimentary free health care. The men or women, and it is mostly the men you see, will stray into an affluent neighborhood and will find an intersection of pedestrian traffic, meaning: near a bakery or small grocery store, and he will become a recognizable fixture. He will stand holding his empty plate. He will speak about the weather, make any amount of small talk to passersby, he won't talk of himself or his life, and he will never overtly demand money. This is how they "beg".

There's no confrontation involved. They await the blessing of charity.

One particular man would sit on the doorstep of my flat. He would always open the door for me, help transport groceries up the winding, turning array of steps, or assist me in any task he could assume a role in completing. He was from Hungary and would return there during apple harvest, for work. He apparently was a hopeless drunk but he was attempting best he could to survive with some sense of dignity.

It was a sad reality to encounter his presence daily. I would give him money at first. Then it was cigarettes. Then bags of bread and cheese. Once he told me that he had relatives in the States and even produced a document denying him a passport as proof of his story. He couldn't speak anything but Hungarian. My expertise in that language was, and still is, lacking.

One day he up and disappeared.

In France, to be homeless is unfortunate but the situation doesn't appear to be as widespread and socially caustic as it is in the U.S. The homeless seem to be few and far between — those who are suffering become regulars that are known to the denizens of a given area. It is perhaps because life on the whole is more condensed and a citizen has a greater opportunity of seeing the same people more often. In short, the homeless are not victims of pure anonymity – they are known faces and thus are linked closer to their surroundings. They become familiars. If one chooses, some type of tenuous relationship can be established, their stories can be known. In the U.S., the homeless comprise an uninteresting factoid as seen on t.v. and as we cross the bad parts of town in our moveable coffins.

Proximity equals empathy. The French tolerate the homeless in a rational way: they provide them with a little dignity and they don't try to feel-good them into changing their chosen lifestyles. That is why the problem there exists, but is not an epidemic.

T.V. LIFE (?)

The shows that are most popular are ones that blatantly peddle nostalgia, romance, and evil seductive combinations of the two. They appear during prime time and last until one a.m. They feature all but forgotten stars of television, film, the stage, whose expertise has dwindled into knowing the answers to the most inane questions adults have ever asked adults. They talk about themselves with too little candor and much too much superfluous personal insight. They talk of their own personal concepts of life, love, eroticism without indulging in the gory details, yet hinting at them. For very lonely viewers, they provide a regular cast of recognizable friends.

At any time during these broadcasts, the participants might break into song. Reasons unknown. They will be tunes only the oldest members of the audience can remember. Unfortunately they are remembered by heart, which causes the viewer him- or herself to uncontrollably sing along. The subject matter: love, love lost, love regained, love lost again. Songs that evoke a better place and time. Songs that are free of any sexual innuendo referring more to a historical event, or generally antiquated thoughts and emotions.

There is also the genre of romantic-voyeuristic programs in which contestants publicly confide more than you've ever wanted to know. Not details of their lovemaking technique, but worse – how they go about enacting their one-man or one-woman theatrical presentations of romance/desire.

One of these shows features three pairs of contestants. Each couple represents two people deeply in love with one another. What the game devises to be unfolds in a series of vignettes and scenarios designed to measure how far, or how much humiliation they can endure, by publicly proving their love. The aim of the competition is for the audience to choose the couple "most in love". It is utterly ridiculous.

Scenes include embarrassing flower deliveries to the female by the man dressed as a giant bunny rabbit (you choose the goofy costume here) at her place of employment. Some episodes measure the reaction of one of the two as they happen upon a billboard, or even skywriting, with a message of the other's love (imagine the surprise!). Often these scenarios are constructed to make one lover look like the biggest fool there ever was while his beloved looks on enthralled. The meaning of this show still eludes.

On the surface: a re-enactment of the mating ritual? Or is it proof that men are proud creatures of romance, i.e. that they are in touch with their feminine selves; that they can dominate culture, art, industry, and fantasy as well? That there is the need to place women on pedestals and give them the gaze of an overlord, for in the show, the female is the ultimate critic.

The apex, zenith, or rock bottom of the program comes with a skin curdling oh-how-we-wish-it-were-karaoke singy song section. The man gets a chance to serenade his beloved on national television. In this gut-wrenching part of the telecast, tears are inevitably shed by all participants: him for her, her for him, both of them in tandem because they can't believe they're doing this in front of millions of viewers, and you, yes, you, the anonymous looker on. Tears of pure cathartic embarrassment. Tears of remembrance of a lost love. Tears envisioning the two after the show in a passionate embrace that their non-stardom has inspired. Tears caused by the wholesale showmanship that true feeling can be boiled down into ratings and marketed. Tears of clowns.

A WALK IN THE CALANQUES

Starting behind the tiny village of Les Goudes because it allows the hiker immediate access to the backcountry and an intersection of civilization and the great outdoors. Les Goudes is on an occasional city bus line so it has a dual nature: isolation with limited linkage to the greater world. Other routes to this large coastal nature preserve lead one straight up the rugged pyramid in ruins of the mountain Marseilleveyre or it will take the uninitiated along a long, winding coastal trek underneath the stoic foreheads of the seaside cliff. The cliff that bookmarks Cassis is the one of the highest sheer drop-offs in all of France.

Les Goudes is the ultimate starting point because it is an uncrowded place that can provide provisions of most types of food and bottled water. The trailhead (a red route as marked on the hiking map to the area) unfortunately is unmarked, or un-signed, in the village. Probably on purpose. It's basically impossible to find: one has to venture down a private alley midway through the stretch of a curving, cliff-perched village, to the tune of barking dogs, and under the glares of the locals trying to figure out your motives for being there. A large rucksack usually aids in non-verbal interpretation. In the alley, houses are on both sides, cats are out front lazily watching for birds with their tails playing snake-charmer in cobras of fur, and little old ladies are out watering their terracotta pots brilliant with red geraniums. At the end of the alley, it is necessary to skirt around the last of the houses, approach what looks like an entrance to someone's backyard because its portal is a seriously drooping clothesline, and a trail under a bower of small palm trees and agave becomes barely apparent. This is the trailhead.

Beyond this initial clump of vegetation, the trail will follow the crease of a tiny corridor-like valley. To the left rise hoodoos that tempt one to scramble up the steep valley side to reach its altar-like position on the hill and climb to the top of the arch in stone it has long since been sculpted into. A distinct possibility on a cool morning. Usually seagulls perch on this arch that is as of yet unnamed. The spine, curdled into fins and teeth, rises to the promontory of Béruveyre, a sub-summit of the more famous Cézanne-portraited older brother. This alternate route leads one up through a burnt forest, past vivid pink outcrops of stone (chemical traces of fire retardant dropped by airplanes), into lushly forested mountainsides and steep valleys that may be descended until you reach their Mayan temple-like jungle surrounded clearings, through needles of stone and steps carved into the hillside, then mostly a steep climb winding up and around a side of a *massif* with few trees and views of the city that show all and tell more. Sea contrails of sailboats can be traced with the eye from these heights and mostly any landmark or neighborhood can be seen in real-time cartography. We're not going that way because the *calanques* promise an escape from known civilization.

The other side of our little initial valley trail is strewn with rusting metal parts, broken bottles, the remains of anonymous machinery, and prickly undergrowth. It's topped by a preternaturally round hill of stone and green bush on which rests the Fortin des Goudes: a miniature medieval fort. The remains have obviously been rebuilt and abandoned, once being the location of an ancient coastal defense perched on such an angular uprise that it is invisible from below.

The end of the valley, blooming with rosemary and thyme and smelling in most seasons like a herbarium is a fallen wall of white tallus. Where it ends upwardly, the trail curves up yet another incline. It must be ascended. After falling up it, or walking on the sides of the crushed rock staircase for better footing, dwarf pines on the hillsides huddle into view, the bones of larger trees have fallen and decorate the landscape in swathes of riddled steel beams eroding, and the sea and her islands loom behind. After only a strenuous twenty-minute climb, the horizon rewards your efforts.

The red trail meets up with the black route. Different colors connote varying difficulties of level: blue = *ridgeline*, green = *perpendicular to peaks*, red = *oblique, switchbacked routes up peaks*, yellow and brown = *ropes will be needed*, black = *along a ledge.* This trail is named *Sentier du Président* and elevates the hike, at the fort's level at two hundred feet above the sea, a distance that sounds small but looks gigantic. What's below is the Mediterranean.

On rounded, downward moving edges of in- and syncline, the landscape takes on a different character, more of someplace in the Aegean. There is the feel of ancient Peloponnesos. The rock underfoot is white. There are pockets of bright red soils spilling from the sides of hills. The *garrigue* is sparse and occurs in clumps of lushness: bush-like scrub that is dark green in color, occasionally flowering with bright pink flowers with even brighter yellow dots in their centers, and all sorts of yellow blooming bush hinting to origins in the Sonoran Desert, not to mention the white to pink blooming heather that is everywhere. The feeling this far into the coastal range is that of venturing far and high into a step-desert with mean, tricky increases of elevation with both sea and forest left remotely behind.

Like a monolith erected for the followers of some ancient religion, the massive wall, erupting in a giant rectangular face, the *Rocher des Goudes*, looms statically in the distance. From different viewing angles it takes on various shapes/meanings. Sometimes: the base of a ziggurat, sometimes: a broken needle tip magnified, sometimes: a cube of sugar. From this point it looks like a severed obelisk. Whatever it resembles, it is ominous, beautiful, and terrifying. On its landward slope it descends into a great sweeping curve of rock, cirque-like, breaking into Half-Moon Pass, then ascending like a funereal monument into the towering cliff of Roc St. Michel – a plateau from which the entire coastal massif can be seen and where it is always very windy.

Underneath these massive formations, any sound from the distance is blocked. Your psyche is free and isolated. All that is heard here are the cries of birds, animals scurrying underfoot, the wind howling through high valleys and passes, and the relentless strum of the sun's waves beating down into the sea's.

As the trail curves around the face of a large foothill made of pure limestone, a descent is begun eastwards and into large amphitheaters of cliff bowls whose floor is covered in wildflowers of mostly yellow varieties, some dwarf pines, the husks of, at one time, shade-providing trees – a bizarre combination of the Sahara and the alpine. The white rocks drip with black and grey watermarks like running mascara. The air burns with the life of vegetation pollinating.

Before taking the next ascent, the Sentier du Club, a white needle is encountered that stands like a totem pole warning of the upcoming increase of heart rate. The uphill climb is mild at first, up a staircase of stone, but the steps don't seem to end – rather, they extend into bigger and bigger, longer and longer gaits leading to an open valley and wall of cliff. The upward goingness is felt but not seen. To the left, spire-like bases of eroding cliffs stand as a landward barrier that conceal further climbing and peaks. The spires themselves can be considered peaks. The view to the right brings in the vast mirror of the sea with its various flowing streamways rippling visible. Marseilleveyre is still an abstracted wall obscuring a view of the city and Les Goudes is all but disappeared. The islands surrounding the village are measurable by the eye. They look forbiddingly desolate and unpeopled. They resemble clouds hardened and stuck in an amber of blue flooded sky.

Although it feels like a major climb, heart reverberating in the throat and ears, the elevation gained is not much more than three hundred feet. What makes it seem much greater is the proximity of these lower elevations to the rapidly climbing crests of one thousand to thirteen hundred feet, underlining it all the base camp of the sea. This combination of extreme natural contrasts magnifies one's senses. It seems vast and endless when it's really small and precious.

Visions appear in the distance: an ancient semaphore on a high crest overlooking Callelongue hangs in the air. Its stone structure built on a rocky fin, with the green-white-blueness, under the shade of low-slung clouds gives it the feel of a desolate Scottish castle (on a sunny day). An eeriness pervades and settles at this elevation.

The first balcony has been reached. Now there is an easy uphill walk shaded by tall pines bleeding a gooey blood of incense. Below the trail is a geologic bowl whose sides are also covered in pine trees, a forest on a mountainside that delivers the solitary walker to the Vallon St. Michel – the valley immediately behind Marseille's final southerly village, Callelongue.

The balcony in places has steps of orange mineralized rock and introduces the hiker to the secret dwelling places of wild bird life. It was from it that I heard my first kestrel squealing like a missile not concerned with reaching a target. The pines are remnants of the huge forest that once existed before decimating fires had begun to be a persistent fact. Their whispers sound like streams emptying. Don't be fooled.

Passing underneath the Tête Trou du Chat, or "Cat hole head" formation, a higher plane is reached. Here, one is face to face with the great rock barrier Roc St. Michel. Its alpine underslopes, or is it the desert, the moon, are intermittently barren and vegetated, with its long monotony broken by the gaping holes of two caves. The Grotte de l'Ours is higher in elevation and easier to attain, if you can follow the confusing orange-green trail confluence. It is immense. The lower cave, Grotte St. Michel d'Eau douce, is reached following a ledge, going down then going straight up a rock face into its perched opening. Both open from a balcony, or actually mountainside shelf, that peers into the valley below and a long tallus staircase of exploded cathedral steps that offers an alternate, extremely difficult, but shorter route up. Climbing tallus is like running up sand dunes that will hurt if you fall on them.

The caves once housed prehistoric men, bears, and who knows what else. They are gigantic, extremely humid, and are longer than the human eye can calculate. What's so wonderful is the fact that they can be explored freely, there's no admission charge, at one's own risk. The risk is great because the humidity, trickling, seeping streams of karst filtration, shallow pools of cool water, and a pervasive mist-like atmosphere make footholds, especially on the trampled soil carpet, a tricky maneuver. Every step is a slippery one and you can't really see where you're going. Flashlights illuminate the way but also cause shadows that play with one's distance perception. The first time I made my way to nearly the end of one, I took votive candles and lit them as I continued my exploration. To have the way out threaded by candlelight helps to postpone the overwhelming claustrophobia that awaits the imaginative mind in each of either cave's haunted galleries.

They contain niches and crystallized ceilings, even a dark lace type of hanging plant. Perhaps there should be some signs for the inexperienced hiker to warn him or her of the dangers inside. They have passages that are relatively easy to descend but not so to get back up and out of. Dark as outer space they tempt one with the sparkling of minerals on their insides. Sadly, many stalagmites and -tites have been chiseled off and taken as souvenirs. These places are beyond time and human construct. Standing at their entrances and looking outward, one feels like the first creature to view the dawn of our being. It looks lonely and harsh out there.

By passing these earthly mysteries this time, we continue around the steep eroded Roc, where the trail does become very hard to follow. It sort of leads to a tallus incline at whose top the trail, now trails, veer off in both opposite and complementary distances. The tallus slope isn't exactly an easier one either.

Several times it'll cause a somewhat winded hiker to fall, and if shade is readily available, it's best to rest a while in it. Its great difficulty tricks one into expending energy to hurry and get the experience over with, but a slow tortuous route conserves muscle power needed for later.

In an attempt to reach the Vallon de la Mounine, presided over by Tête de la Mounine, we pause. We think about how foreign the word "mounine" is and remember the laughs it garnered when we asked a local what it signified. It is a Provençal word for the private parts of a female. Why, or how a mountain crest came to be named this is worthy of some meditation in the clear air.

Considering some of the names that surround the hiker: there's the Plateau of the Dead Man, Half-Moon Pass (*Pas de la Demi-Lune*), there's the Deserter's Cave, Cave of the Column, Goat Pass, both small and large Bad Valleys, Valkyrie Woods; there are the formations Cat Jump, Tower of Pisa, The Candle and the Candle Bowl; a spring called Pork Well, there's the Glass Eye Calanque, Camel Island, Window Valley; there's a naturally occurring version of the Great Wall of China (*Muraille de Chine*), Saddle Woods, the Crab Claws, Donkey Foot Valley, Black Cross Valley, Bloody Valley, Grindstone Head, a seaside valley called the Sixty-Four Contours, the Fountain of Truth, the Finger of God, Louis' Cave, the Bay of Hells, American Promontory, Torpedo Island, the Stairs of Giants, Monkey Bay.

Having ventured this far into the Massif de Marseilleveyre, one is either well on a way in or in a whole heap of trouble. There isn't any drinking water available, unless the few wells, called *puits*, hold small green pools infested with tadpoles. The sea glimmers in the unreachable distance that really doesn't look that far away. It's blindingly bright when the sun intersects it, deep blue and calm. On days that the sea is agitated by storms or the mistral, waves spike its surface in myriad shark fins of white crest.

Forsaking an attempt at the peak of Marseilleveyre, a mere thirteen hundred vertical feet above sea level, its imaginary ascent can be documented here in quick time.

There's a vertical rock face that I once conquered with my German shepherd puppy (not exactly small) in my backpack. It's thirty to fifty feet straight up and a little sideways and probably one of those places one might not want to look down from. After this task, there's a high valley, for the *calanques* are really a series of valleys superimposed upon each other and separated by striations of bone, featuring scrub growth so lush that one can picnic in its shade. The view, at this higher elevation, reveals Les Goudes in all its model railroad village ramshackle splendor and humble, timid collection of human souls in the midst of jagged, blustery nature. The view also encompasses the deserted islands of Jaïre and Riou.

They resemble some sort of combination of surfacing submarine made of salt and a never before known dinosaur's array of dorsal fins. They are tips of ridges exiled into a displacement from the land that serves to heighten their difference. During the machinations of the sun throughout the day, they'll be colored and shaded in weird bands of bright and darkness. Specks of the remnants of vegetation they once grew remain detectable to the eye. They look like UFOs in stop motion, cloud stone, the jaws of a mythical beast, always enigmatic and foreboding. It's a tragedy that their once thick wigs of pine have been harvested hundreds of years ago when conservation wasn't an issue. What is left is a tortured sculpture of erosion's oeuvre.

The sea life below their uncontaminated shores is another story. Rarely are these islands visited. Around them pop out singular rocks that only birds care about. However, one of these forgotten places contains an arch of entry that faces the sea. Ducking heads in a small boat and carefully entering this unknown port reveals a circular ruin of walls surrounding an arbitrary pool of sea. The walls climb to about fifteen feet, so it makes for a great hidden cove to go rock diving. Of course the uninhibited sea is tens of degrees cooler this far out.

Why these places remain unknown/unharassed by humanity is the basic fact that they have nothing to offer. All one can do on them is be utterly alone, often with no view of anything even remotely human, except passing ferries, and experience what it feels like to live as an existentialist à la Beckett. To be the last or first conscious being aware. There aren't many takers for such a ride.

After imagining what island life is like, the sound of rushing wind returning the scent of reality, there's a long, steadily uphill hike to be made during which the temperature might decrease by a few degrees. Clouds blow by overhead that can be hit with a thrown rock. There's one more difficult rock face to conquer, so vertical that the hiking club has drilled-in steel ropes into its surface to lend a helping boost of stability. It's completely necessary to use them on the way down.

The peak of Marseilleveyre offers boundless views and probably the best place to look back on the continent from southern France. All of Marseille can be seen in the bare nudity of its existence, then the bay of Marseille, then the mountains and hill that ferociously hem in the city and separate it from anywhere else in the world, let alone France. On superbly clear days, and there are many each month, one can see as far north as Mount Ventoux, northeast to Ste. Baume with its glinting observatory, to the southerly dollop of rock that hides the port of Toulon. Views that are reminiscent of classical etchings of Naples or Rome. See the top of Marseilleveyre and live forever.

The peak offers up some interesting ruins: a giant cross (as there are on all mountain tops in the south of France), and on windy days or portions of the afternoons clouds scratch their bellies on the summit. When I was last there, I stood on an outcrop, steadied myself, face into the wind, and for the first time ever, I ate cloud.

To view Marseilleveyre and to photograph or paint it as Cézanne did is homage. To experience as it is, is to climb it. In attaining its reasonable heights, it disappears under the feet and rises like an altar over the city it protects and defines.

Bypassing its splendid singularity, it's off to Pine Pass. There's a small *abri* here – a shelter naturally occurring in stone (sometimes they're built of wood) – a place to wait out a storm or hide from the rays of sunshine. The pass is vertically U-shaped and horizontally shaped like a bowl. Its sides are overgrown in pines and it has the feel of another otherworld, a forest paradoxically springing from beds of tallus hemmed by low-growing scrub.

Resembling an alien landscape characteristic of early Star Trek episodes, this place is oddly magical, familiar, remote. Greenness, whiteness, greyness of shade and colors coloring. A jagged cereal bowl of mountains. Window through which the beyond is, including blue margin of sea. Cliffs of stone chimneys waiting patiently to smoke. One hill reachable only with great exertion pitted with tiny caves, the houses of birds? No, they contain miniature dunes of red sand and a few crystals. Buddha caves that await someone to fill them with scroll poems.

From this elevated point, a downward trek takes one through a dry valley whose formations and elongation brings memories of southwestern American deserts. This desolate charming route winds underneath the far side of Roc St-Michel through the Mounine Valley, under vertical faces on either side that stare at nothing in particular except elements white and blue in flux, far from a wall in the distance that is the Plateau of the Dead Man whose underbelly is of broken tooth upliftings that only a foolhardy climber would dare to floss. At a lower level poses the raised contour of the Mounine Massif.

Pausing in the valley for water or a snack is highly recommended. Even though there's a lack of trees, the jutting formations provide walls of shade. There's ever the option of climbing to the next ridge, going due east, paralleling the sea, with a tour of all the *calanques* in mind, destination Cassis. Not too good of an idea unless it's a cool month without rain. In the spring and summer, the heat is impenetrable and debilitating. It fills your lungs with humidity and sautés the skin.

If the high road is taken, it will lead to the Galinette Pass where's there's an outcrop that looks as if it's formed of crystal. There are pockets of red soil and veins of sparkling minerals and fully formed crystals that can be easily mined from the earth surrounding. Please, take only a few. The stone around this corner ridge is well worn and feels like drip stone to the touch. It's an acre of otherworldliness and rugged beauty. It appears on no maps.

*

Heading southeasterly down the Mounine Valley the scenery completely changes. Above it, embedded in the cliff face are more habitable caves. Cave of the Deserter is quite small and cozy and is arrayed in every shade of orange that soil can be translated into. It's abandoned, not even garbage or bonfires' burnt-out clutter mar its interior. A lovely, lonely place with views of marching cliffs aligned in regiments, walking towards the sea.

The valley is amazingly lush. Entering its bowels, you must drop down a vertical of about ten feet with the assistance of fractured rock perfect for foot/handholds. Even on detailed hiking maps the thin stream of forest this valley conceals is undetectable. Scrub bushes grow to twice the height of a human. With the psychological reservation one feels when entering a dark wood, the trail sinks into leafy greenness. It feels as if you've mis-turned and are walking into a dead end of vegetation. You must bend, crouch into the cool shady darkness because not enough hikers pass through to keep this part of the trail pruned. After maneuvering through the unkempt branches, and after a few scratches (but aren't all introductions painful?), you have entered a bower.

The trees are almost as those in parks. The trail gradually begins to widen. There are boulders eager to be used as lounge chairs. There's the sound of water trickling, which might be an illusion or not. Certainly the foliage indicates a flowing stream (probably underground). In the midst of arid cliffs and wind blown peaks, hellish escalators of tallus constantly running downwards, the forest primeval sways lowly and pulsates green.

Sea breezes invade the valley and cool the sweat that the body wears like a tight cloak.

In the secret forest, there's nothing to be done but to rest. It's perfect for picnicking in or even napping. Its dimensions of cover and shade are tame: it's about two hundred yards long and twenty wide. It's enough and incongruously enough to transport the soul (again!). A landscape entirely unexpected: the trees aren't pines but those of deciduous nature. It feels like a hardwood forest of northern climes.

Paradise unfortunately can only be enjoyed for a quick eternity. Coming out of the breezy bower there are long tallus descents. Always there's the philosophical quandary: is it easier going up or down? The best way to descend is to avoid total prudence. Do not worry about each footfall. If you slide and fall, the backpack and your butt will save you from injury. The method for coming down tallus slopes is to go with the flow: run, sort of pounce downward using the feet as skis. Of course it's very hard on the legs, shins, and ankles, but what is being used is the very nature of tallus in an attempt to defeat its inherent difficulty. It absorbs your weight while it propels you down its slope. Stopping, though, is a matter of individual interpretation.

Towards the end of the valley, its canyons lean in a steep twenty to sixty foot rise that provide balconies where it is tempting but impossible to set up camp. The pine needle-blanketed earth rests in beds tilting at nearly ten percent grade. Rarely can one tell this fact until hiking up to a prospective clearing. Pine trees do abound shading the way and perfuming the salty sea air with the incense of alpine freshness.

On days when the sea blows clouds into these desolate valleys — if there is some kind of consciousness in them to

observe the grey-ing of air, stone, cloudbank, tops of trees —
what will occur is the transformation of a normally sunny, semi-
arid massif dreaming the tropics into a landscape
indistinguishable, for moments, from that of the Hautes Alpes.

Coming down the Mounine Valley, pines overgrow the trail
semaphoring the hiker to stop and climb, or rest in, their thick
sturdy branches. Some trees will even dare you to hang upside
down from their low cradles of everlasting wood and goodsmell.
Like Jungle Jims growing from the chalky earth, they ask to stop
for a while and come play.

The valley opens onto the sea and the two floating lunar
landscapes of Ile Jaron and Ile Jaïre. Devil's islands they are
sporting tortured toothy, horny white formations that only
shapeshift and appear weirder with proximity.

Barren, with mature, rock-clinging vegetation that resembles
tundra, a total absence of trees, inhabited once by wildlife such as
rabbits, fox, eyed lizards, and goats, (now populated only with
the bones of goats), blue rock thrush, Bonelli's eagles, and
patrolled by wild flocks of chatty seagulls, what good are these
desolate places?

To be completely alone with one's nerves.

To participate within the natural world's world.

To view life in abstraction, how it moves, revolves, is
enlivened by moveable stasis.

To inhabit ever briefly a deserted isle.

To get away from getting away from it all.

To understand why our moon is named with seas.

To view a continent's diminished perspectives of inter-
colliding planes.

To be detached, alone, to know that death is full of life.

To reach the islands a boat must be taken. This is not the case for the Ile Maïre which is just off a peninsular spine extending from the hamlet of Les Goudes. This is a formidable landform. It looks like a giant smiling, half-submerged skull. To get to it a turgid bay-like corridor must be swum, not in itself a Herculean task (unless you happen to be wearing shoes) but a dangerous one because, from a set of eyes at water and wave level, distance is made irrelevant. At any time a speedboat may rip through the narrow seaway, as many do, stirring up the waters with two-foot waves, and these waves can easily conceal a human treading water. From time to time the small *calanques* around Les Goudes collect the mincemeat made of unlucky tuna or dolphins.

Once the water corridor is crossed and the swimmer is dizzy with the elation of reaching and passing the midway point, an approachable port to the island must be found. The waves are tumultuous and the rocks surrounding the island's base are sharp and studded with urchins and there are no silver pool handlebars to latch onto. Happily, there is an old stairway made of concrete that has been constructed into the rocky coastal lip. It begins two to four feet above the water and is surrounded by a rocky bay whose shallow floor is observable from the surface. It's not easy to get to the steps but it is probably the best place to try. Sometimes humankind's abandoned infringement on nature has some benefit.

Once having pulled myself up from the rudely boisterous sea, and having rested on the steps to view the mainland from which I was isolated, swarms of seagulls welcomed me. They do this by diving at your head and screaming vociferously. It's a scene that would give Hitchcock goose bumps. Most likely, they won't connect with the cranium, but it's best to toss up a rock in their general direction every once in a while. It is so strange to see their aggressive dive-bombing and it lets one know how rarely mammals disturb their outpost of paradise.

The trails there are ill-marked and not well worn. They need to be re-invented. Really there's only one: it crosses the island's balcony over the sea, heads inland, up and down through a small valley, then up a winding ascent that leads to another staircase that leads to the Seagull Peak, Pic des Gabians. On my way up I was startled to see the dried-up husk of a goat's body, perhaps better described as an unwrapped mummy.

At the outcrop that presides over all, there's a ruin of an ancient observatory. Remade of rusted steel and resembling either the scrap metal of cargo ships or a World War One fortification, it's a spooky place to view the mind-reeling panoramas which envelop. It's a platform of rust and metallic decay whose interior is full of burnt wood and human refuse. The cliffs that it overlooks gradually descend into ridge tops and the outstretched leg of the islands lower to more rugged elevations. The mainland-facing side is sheer cliff. A suicide of elevation. The sea beneath is regularly a cold-boiled broth of turbulence made by tide and storms.

But the sea underneath is pristine. Around this island, spearfishing competitions are held due to the vast amounts of fish and the clarity of the waters. Dives made here are frigid and frothy and wildly pristine. It's another world that few ever venture into even though it's so close to a metropolis and completely attainable. Guess it's better that way.

Backtracking, backtracking, shimmying through switch-backs, rediscovering where it is we are: viewing the islands which our spirits will journey to later as eager Ulysses. The Calanque de la Mounine is far enough extracted from civilization as to be soul-purgingly exotic. On the mainland across the straits, it contains a tiny sliver of beach that is easily hiked to, or one can descend into it on steps of limestone. A good part of the best hiking months it'll be occupied by tired walkers rejuvenating, families (they hike together in France!), or bathers who deem this spot worthy of the long coastal trek from Callelongue they must take to reach it.

Under its clear, clean water, there are vertical rockfaces covered in nothing and darkened black by salt. Ten feet deep sea urchins abound. Fifteen to twenty feet bright orange starfish begin waving their pickled orange hands, schools of fish swim by undisturbed, then in a flash of metallic lightning, they turn catching sun. Twenty feet and below tuna dart by touting their sharpened fins and octopuses grasp and let go of rotundities of current.

From the Calanque de la Mounine, we head east along the coast towards a destination point. Skirting the bottom of a three hundred foot steep pyramid of a peak and walking onto a hardened lip that separates sea from the inclines behind, the plane below the trail is one of several labyrinths of jagged rock welded together. Partially covered in scrub that is extremely low-lying. The vegetation here, with not any observable soil to cling to, resembles a forest of bonsai. Beyond the strangely reduced treeline the shore appears to be flat, what the British call a shingle, but approaching it, one is introduced to a rock hopper's paradise of tiny canyons and cliffs that if misstepped can easily snap a limb.

Tiny, flattened outcrops jut from the sea, islets that sort of resemble the greens of rundown miniature golf courses. They tempt one to swim to them out of curiosity perhaps in an effort to feel what it's like to be a seagull. The moving tears in the sea around them indicate that the tide here is king. The islets provide channels in which the currents and tide can torque. Normally not a threat, the open sea combined with the high number of urchins, an increased tide, factor in the unknown of the vast expanse of dream (or is it nightmare?) blue adds up to a danger not worth taking. There are many places out here that no one goes.

This coastal area deep into the calanques is great for finding a niche, proclaiming it as one's own territory by placing a backpack on a high point, and within its walls of privacy, salt smell, sea view, abstracted remoteness, the opportunity to sunbathe in the buff is unavoidable. If this is not what France is for, what Europe is about, what any natural paradise offers, then it's all for nothing.

The sea urchins do make skinny dipping a challenge and most people of non-Mediterranean extraction will find it awkward to reveal all on the crowded city beaches. Here, there's a certain *calanque* for nudists, Sugiton, but really one can be free in a million or so places far from the discerning eyes of others.

Walking around the outcrop known as the Roche Percée there are many opportunities to climb its sides into coverings of mature pine, into enclosures that provide seats of white limestone and carpets of fresh pine needles and cones. These are great places to escape the heat, to picnic, or to take a siesta. Where to set up camp without really having to set up camp. Mushrooms, so close to the sea, in a thin stratum of soil spring from the floor daring you to pick them.

Beyond our destination point is perhaps a better destination: the *Callanque de Marseilleveyre*. Surrounded by an embankment of stone and anchored in brightly colored soil, this dream cove hides a large crescent-shaped sand beach that is rarely if ever peopled by a crowd. There's a restaurant run by a family who lives in pure isolation, except in the summer months. For the going rate, one can get dinner, drink, desserts in the middle of an incredibly beautiful, subtropical no-man's-land of distinct Grecian derivation.

No more than two or three small boats are allowed to dock here and the shallowness of the bay makes it impossible for the bigger ones to get near. This very genuine outpost of civilization happily lost is decorated by the ruins of an ancient *batterie,* or defense, on an overlooking coastal promontory. Someone during some recent expanse of time planted rows and clumps of agaves which continue to this day to bloom from their white green and yellow striped prickly artichoke cores. Fist-sized rocks jewel either side of the beach to placate erosion. The best thing about it is that there's no heretofore reference to it to be found – not in books, guides, magazines, or even today's information pornography of the Internet. It's a secret that will exist long after secrets are kept.

Most people who do discover this cove are those who travel by water on small pleasure craft. Hiking long distance is somewhat of a rarity these days, but occasionally one will find women, walking painfully in high heels. They come for a pre-lunch visit and can't resist, lured by the coastline. The French aren't as gear-oriented as Americans. Dressing up for nature isn't for them a contradiction in terms.

Due west, hidden and available only to the adventurous, is a geological formation, our destination, the Théâtre. It's an embankment overlooking the sea. It might have been something else once, not man-made, but something celebrated by the numerous agaves planted safely in the land just above it. No one knows what its origins are – it's a true geologic theater in the midst of the *massif,* where the land ends and cups the sea. It's better that no one knows or cares about it anymore.

What it looks like is this: a cliff ending in distance, from an overlooking perspective. Below its cliché of edge, for the few who dare walk the few meters off the trail to the nothing it promises lies a rippling stratification of multicolored beach caves. It looks like a cranium split open with its brains drained out. It could be Neanderthals' first lodge.

No vegetation could grow on its icebergs of stone. Minerals accreting and replicating within the caves paint hues of orange, yellow, red, green, grey, purple, crimson, rust, metallic blues and blacks. Almost impossible to tread upon with bare feet, the waters surrounding must be swum with great care. The waves here, unimpeded by landmasses or breakers, are many times the strength of those lazily eroding the city beaches. Unless scuba diving, their forces in sound and fury and spray blatantly prohibit one entering, especially on a blustery day.

There are approximately four distinct cave formations. Most are more hospitable to crab life. One, facing eastwards, allows a crevice of sharpened rock that is gradually inclined enabling a cautious approach to the water. Behind it is its overhang deep enough for shelter from the sun or a sudden sea storm. Its floor is not at all smooth and is clammy to the touch.

The waters under these caves when not roiling in salt, sand, and leftover mistral energy transferred to current are usually somewhat wavey and mind-numbingly clear. Partially sandy at the sea floor, strewn with fields of boulders and monoliths, outcrops of limestone that serve now as walls for desolate cities of seaweed fields growing in an attempt at civilized unison, it all is necessarily explorable. Not too far from here caves that contained prehistoric painting were discovered. Who knows what waits to be found below. Below, it is dark, dark.

What's beyond the immediate sunken boulder fields is hard to discern. More fields of sand that are oasied by large tree top-like clumps of seaweed called Halimeda. It resembles a desert/scrub landscape – only submerged. And the water gets deeper, heavier, murkier. These clumps of seaweed in a rippled, barely moving desert seascape promise a design of infinity. They tempt a diver/snorkeler to follow, promising discovery, then offering an indistinct, untraceable way back. One can only go so far out before losing any sense of direction and line of shoreline perspective. It's the closest some might ever get to flying.

Looking back and invoking the sin of looking back into the breaking waves, head above water, the surface cuts itself into units of flux, never even attempting to suggest stability, the coast and the cliffs tower over in an illusion of tiny distance, as in a very realistic section of a diorama. What they are is unreachable. What's seen just below are the gaping mouths of the caves, a promontory, and seaward, islands. The sea's eternity of endless green/blue tells you when you are here: there is nowhere in life to turn. There is no one to be and the closest we might ever come to our roots is in this soup of being all of humanity has lurched itself out of.

The caves are home to small rock crabs that, like their surroundings, are colored with grey, blue, and dark red carapaces. They scurry away as soon as they sense they're being watched. Try as one might, they're impossible to catch unless they're found sidestepping through a shallow underwater inlet. Rarely will they pinch, even when hiding in the fleshy palm of a curious hand.

On the sandy inlet floors, sea snails suction cup across rockfaces, and like sunken, bloated cigars, sea cucumbers lie in stasis. They grow up to a foot long and nearly three inches thick. They are slimy, dark purple, unabashedly phallic and in no way can they be called charming. But they bother no one. Out of pure interest, they should be brought up to the surface where they'll inevitably emit a squirt gun stream of seawater and they'll crinkle their bodies like quickly drying fruit.

Scuba gear is required to dive deep enough underwater to view veins of glowing red coral, psychedelic colored sea slugs, large octopuses, and grouper fish. Ten or so meters out from the coastline in the Théâtre's waters, the casual snorkeler will spot schools of fish and perhaps even a white-topped trumpet anemone. Slow floats just above a bed of rocks might offer a glimpse of a peacock worm: it lives in a tube that can lengthen up to six inches. What sprouts from the cylinder's end is a braided, fan-shaped galaxy of tendrils that are brightly banded, reminiscent of a sun made of fleshy strings. When it senses a presence, it sucks itself into disappearance.

The *calanques* around the Théâtre will occasionally be stocked with cuttlefish bones. When alive and swimming, these zebra-striped relatives of the octopus with their kinte cloth turbans look like sea crafts straight out of Jules Verne.

Fan mussels, living Babylonian ornamentation with little horsetails of filaments, reach lengths of three feet. They're a rarity. The best-known fish of the immediate area is the *Rascasse.* There are boats and restaurants that take its name. I have never seen one so it remains a secret or mundanity of lore. Translated, it means "scorpion fish". As one native explained it to me: "It's reddish, not too big, spiny with an ugly face, sharp teeth . . ."

The Théâtre is a theater for absolutely nothing except sun worship, swimming, and total isolation from the community that is humanity. It's where one can find the secret existence often conceals: the appreciation of the senses and the abandonment of all that is sensible. Not to paint a desert island picture of what it does and does not encompass, for just beyond it is a restaurant whose views must contain thousands of paintings the Impressionists or Expressionists never attempted. The Théâtre leaves it up to you.

Mountains are diminished into wave line; mountain ranges are stacked into non-parallel lines of cathedral steps without a place of worship but the sky. Clouds more resemble mountains and extend for distances that are unearthly, more characteristic of Jupiter or Saturn. The sea as endless or infinitely finite rock garden of water that extends beyond the use of boundaries. The sea allowed to be the enigma it is without hiding a thing defined by the underlined thesis of what it's not. Its surface a liquid element meeting air element diffused with earth element meeting air element in a bowl of fire that is being. The land that rests stoically behind is a wall of matter that doesn't really matter, a barrier from the everywhereness the sea suggests.

From anywhere within the Théâtre the view looking beyond is a perspective bent necessarily inward. Go there once and you'll never return.

Toy boX

Each morning the shutters must be opened, shutters that are as big and unwieldy as doors. Held back by hinged doorstop devices attached to the walls outside, each opening celebration is accompanied by a loud, painful *creeeeeeaaaak* in both the shutter's hinge and the hinges of the body that's doing the opening. When they're opened, daylight and the city's operetta of sound is welcomed. Shutters shut leave inhabitants with no idea of the conditions outside – hardly a drop of light is let in through them. Shutters caught in the wind can do thousands of francs of damage. Caretakers against the forces of weather, humans soon become the caretakers of shutters. The daily ritual of opening and nightly vespers of closing them gives one a sense of control over the greater powers that be just outside the molting windowsills. Personae made by the architecture that frames them.

Will the chain-pull toilet be working today? is always the question somewhere lurking in the worry lobes of the brain. Some of these devices have signs posted next to them: *Do not pull hard.* The well of flushing water is raised seven feet above the seat. Lesser miracles are worked when its plumbing doesn't leak on the occupant below. The bathroom's pagan atmosphere is further exemplified by that other toilet seat never occupied for too long.

The bidet is the lower body's sink. It may double for a basin to wash clothes in, a playful child's urinal, a porcelain foot washing pool, or a temporary home for goldfish suffering the indignity of a bowl cleaning. Why Americans fear the bidet so is for the reason that it reminds us we don't clean ourselves as resolutely as most of the rest of the world does.

In the attic, the rain reservoir goes mostly unchecked, unthought of. When it storms, the roof not designed to be completely watertight filters streamlets of rain into a concrete basin. The water is used either as a back up emergency supply or in very old buildings as a source. Hopelessly outdated they are nevertheless kept around because they are too cumbersome to remove.

The spillway built into the slightly tilted terrace empties as best it can into a drain pipe that on nights of parties inevitably gets emptied into by human rainstorms. It's too easy not to pee into. After a downpour or a cleansing by hose, graceful erosional sediments mimic the patterns of what sand naturally does at the beach: eddies undone, alluvial fans of windblown silt, birds' feathers, leaves, the remains of pigeons' late-night snacks collect on the terrace and slowly spill in waterslides leaving signatures of gravity. Moraines of daily existence.

Skylights that in forgotten passageways to the roof's upper terrace are rarely taken care of properly (cleaned) and the natural light they so freely give is taken for granted, filtered by dust and filmy layers of smoke. Hardly does anyone ever even look up at them to gauge the sky's current current of blue, greyness, white. Encased in a bubble or behind a plane of glass as seen from the roof and a thin sheet on its underbelly (the ceiling of the room illuminated), these passages are limbolands for the collections of cobwebs, plaster mortified, and the occasional coin or child's toy dropped from within the corps of the structure that superstitious builders deposited in the mortar for luck.

These skylight passageways hear generations of laughter, fights, and joy as they're fogged over by countless clouds of cooking fumes while they're only remembered or appreciated when, in their great age, they leak tears of having been forgotten. What they can see is the yellow and blueish glimmers of dwarf irises blooming in the hills that city dwellers consider "so far away."

No one homE

An intersection Y-shaped. Billboards that change so often it's hard to remember what they were advertising, but the face of the man who re-pastes it is like a friend's. Glass closets of phone booths that serve a clientele around noon and then six o'clock. Sometimes there's a line whose members can't help themselves waiting, crushing cigarette butts with their heels, finally, tapping on the outside barrier to let a greedy caller know that it's time to get out.

Just before the street breaks into a long lonely boulevard taken mostly by buses and drivers who, in speeding off to work, take the long way to avoid traffic, past a field growing lettuce and cabbage outlined with concrete irrigation canals, with sad apartments on either of the road's sides, behind a crumbling wall, is a house.

No one lives in the house and the ground it occupies in its zoo cage of overgrown weeds, trees that have never been pruned, virgin patches of original grassiness that serve as a reminder of what has everywhere else been paved over. Bamboo grows out of control and is ripe with its fruit of discarded garbage. Butterflies spawn in humid shadiness, beauty like leaves in apotheosis.

The house looks nearly habitable: it still has its tile roof intact, the walls aren't in such ill repair, there's a pile of bricks under a window waiting to help out, and someone has planted a tomato garden in a tame corner of its wilderness.

At night when I have the courage to leap the wall, I approach and knock on its sagging door. A cat leaps out the window almost taking flight. I rummage through the refuse inside, with a flashlight, searching for evidence of why I am there.

THE SITTING

She wonders what life is like in Kansas today. If trees still grow stories high above the white farmhouse whose floors are in a slump and whose eaves are inhabited by more birds than her brother could ever hope to pick off with his BB gun. She wonders if cows are standing at the fence as they are wont to, waiting to have what's left of the vegetables and skins of fruit delivered to them just for their big wet pink noses asking. She wonders if Joséphine will be at the *boucherie* four thousand three hundred miles from where her thoughts are today so that she might ask her as she does every other day for the plumpest rôtisserie chicken which she'll share over the next few days with her dog who in its old age must pee on newspapers carpeting the halls of the three-tiered house. She wonders what she'll do this season for money: be a tour guide for some sporadic wealthy travelers from the States (many wives of doctors) who invade her secluded world to offer her their unconcealed ignorance and news of the country that she, like a lover, almost fell in love with, so out of desperation, abandoned. She wonders when it will stop raining and if it's the sound of the drops on her windows that she has never even once washed that is making her feel this way. She wonders when she'll ever have guests again, being lonely for the loneliness of company, escaping from her visitors when they come by practicing the piano or reading books very slowly in her bedroom, looking out her window at the one small mountain she can see that hides from her everything her life has ever been.

Borély

Walking through its southern, uncelebrated entrance, you enter a Greek temple. There's a courtyard with a monolith centering the space – on top of the monolith are two heads, Janus-style, its named carved underneath: Eurythemes.

Men distribute their families in the courtyard of the city park and force them to act as a short-lived audience for their impending games of *boules;* women sit on benches talking about anything and everything and happily don't watch. On one side of the courtyard that is a field of leveled tan gravel, there's a wrought iron fence that keeps safe an ancient mossy fountain and some fallen pillars of ruins probably as recent as the 18th or 19th centuries. Antiquity kept behind bars.

The château that presides over the courtyard dates from the eighteenth century and normally houses a museum of artifacts. It has been closed to the public for far too long, awaiting renovations. At least one family, or a solitary caretaker, lives inside, for there is discernible life fidgeting behind an expanse of shutters. And there is laundry hanging from them to be dried.

Hardened arteries of pines ripple from the ground near the children's play area. There are some cheap carnival rides, a small merry-go-round. Sad faux organ sounds keeping mechanical time counterpointed by crying and screaming. Youth's rage for life.

Beyond the château is its grand entranceway resplendent in flowing staircases that pour around a water-filled basin with fountain. Stretching for hundreds of yards in front of the fountain are manicured lawns planted with flowerbeds. Faithful joggers circumambulate around these lawns on which children chase soccer balls or around which they race the runners, pedaling like crazy their bulky rented bicycles.

Outlining the lawns is a racetrack of gravel, what used to be the château's driveway for carriages. Adults too rent the large, steel-framed pedal-driven rickshaws. They seat up to five, so the two pedallers in front do all the work. Outings on these contraptions habitually and with clockwork regularity crash into trees or curbs or other bicycles. They are easily steered out of control when their frightened pilots approach the park's one mild slope.

Of course, they must be evacuated by all passengers when uphilling the slope. This is especially true, but not believed by the leagues of poor sons-in-law who try to transport their cargoes of overweight mothers-in-law and pregnant wives up the little hill that to them quickly becomes a rounded-off Everest. Watching the weekend bicyclers provides a vaudeville of how social relations will either collide or in some way stall.

The rest of the park is a woodland wound with trails. There are hidden nooks of imaginary campsites and paradises of shade cooler by pools of water. Paths, some paved, some covered in gravel, some dried tongues of mud wind through isolated clumps of forest that one can almost get lost in. The woods conceal hiking trails that mountain bikers use as quick weekend getaways. A water spider's skating rink.

On the northeasternmost corner, behind the botanical and rose gardens, there's a shaded tunnel paved by a dirt boulevard that leads to a statue of Diana on the hunt. She looks over a gorge that is filled with a shallow creek, the river L'Huveaune, which is usually tepid and drained of all current but a trickle.

The pleasant wooded fields on the other side of the gorge hide Roland Petit's famous dance school. Emptying into the sea, the creek river widens into an inlet creased and folded into rocky coastal limestone – a tiny bay where kayak enthusiasts gather. The natural canal leading from dry gorge to impatient sea runs under the north, main entrance to the park where there are a few food stands and long chaotic lines of bicycles rented and returned. This area is constantly peopled with innocent revelers during the day while the night brings out ladies of the evening.

The park's interior is shaded by plane trees, one of which rises sixty feet into the heavens. Its branches are evenly spaced scimitars that tempt the daring to climb to its highest perch. This tree presides over a field of its own. The wealth of trees, at first look, keeps the man-made lake at the park's center a well-kept secret. The lake is large and features a bird island and a human island that can be reached via footbridge. On this latter faux isle, there's a faux glacier offering a small variety of sandwiches and ice cream: snacks priced at four times their value, but then it's the scenery that's truly being rented.

The lake extends around this island in a narrow channel that provides a navigational challenge for those not used to rowing and steering. This tree- and bush-lined channel is held in high regard by flocks of migratory and residential birds. It's a regular nesting place for the park's ducks and swans, a few roosters and chickens too, as it allows them all to escape the crowds with their bags of bland, stale bread.

The tiny channel artfully does what it's meant to do: mimic in miniature the Loire valley or make boaters and those strolling feel as if they are on a famous French canal. It's soul-refreshing.

Other points of interest: a fountain constructed to resemble a cave, dripping with beards of moss with a pool swum by hungry non-koi pond fish (they'll eat the bread!). A person-sized reproduction of an Armenian cross looking quite Celtic in decor and design. Statues of once famous dignitaries gesturing to something just off in the moving waves of leaves. The remains of World War II bunkers growing anything that will try to cover them up, to invade their memory boxes with vegetal forgetfulness. Paths that wind in and out of people, families partaking in and enjoying this public airing of who they are. Women in what Americans might think of as their "Sunday best" when really it's how they usually dress, talking to other women standing in semi-circles of interest, their shoes kicked off, their bright white feet grooming the grass. Children running everywhere because it's the one place they are allowed to be wild yet they are polite enough to diminutively ask you to retrieve a ball they got stuck in the tree under which you are dreaming. People exercising and watching other people exercise, which is an exercise in the civility of desire. The lake caked in places with floating bread that the spoiled, pampered birds will eat only out of boredom, if at all. The music of the children's rides drifting the day away in the absence of any responsible thoughts. Air cooled by sea breezes, swirling, swirling, swirl –

OLD NEWS, NO NEWS

Considering the language barrier, an all too real invisible concept that, with simple body movements, can be, and is constantly broken through, the consistently unfair rate of currency exchange always in the bank's favor, the challenge of navigating a city built on a street and autoroute schematic rooted in civil disobedience/confusion, a bureaucracy that no longer takes pleasure in its straight-faced orders invoking hundreds of steps, several of which might be to prove one's existence, whose documentation in triplicate needs to be stamped with actual lickable stamps not for mailing but of government approval that cost a phenomenal fee, to be then followed by further Byzantine procedures that have developed circuitousness to a High Art, the inability to park anywhere one might need to be at any given time, the host of tiny social inflections that either pave the way to approval or barricade oneself from functioning "normally" within the greater good of peoplehood, weighing the quotidian challenge of remembering the right vocabulary word memorized once in a dimly lit hall of the academy so that when you walk to the local bricolage and ask for "batteries" you don't accidentally ask for "pills" (*piles/pillules*) if merely to avoid the conversation tangent such an incidence will stir up, learning how to pronounce the names of American cigarettes in French because French ones are too strong so that you won't be corrected when asking for Lights as "Leets" when the vendor, attempting English says it

"Lyghtes, vous ne le savez pas?" as if he were himself from Virginia, through the thick and thin of it, after a hard day's coping as a foreigner, there's the wonderful gift of the evening news. Sometimes, pictures of the States, but mostly anywhere else but . . . as the commentators and experts and newspeople banter about so speedily, so perceptively, so intellectually that not a word is comprehensible. Deliverance.

WAITRESSES

Typically your waitron in France will be a man. Mature, suave, well-groomed, and occasionally well-mannered and easygoing. Typically, women abide by the mores of a sexist country: they may keep bar as they are more reluctant to hand out free drinks while their presences entice and lengthen the tabs of friendly, amorous drunks. One thing's for sure: most bars contain a 10:1 male to female ratio.

One will find women in the kitchen producing the meals, which in France, regardless of where lunch or dinner is taken, are gourmet. They might be the bussers of your table, the sweepers and moppers of floors, but rarely will they wait tables.

When this rarity does occur it is quite plain that they are the most beautiful waitresses in the world. Why this is so boldly true is found almost singularly in their comportment. They hold themselves as you would want to. Hair pulled back in a bun with a few strands falling on their inhumanely high cheekbones, whose textures are not masked by make-up, that they blow away again and again throughout the day with puckered lips you shall never ever ever kiss. Shoes with heels that lengthen their frames tipping the balance and giving them a stature of power, keeping them high above the most excellent tables of food decorated by dishes a chef has prepared resembling more modern decorative art than plates of stuff to be eaten.

They smell of dinner and perfume and a hint of perspiration. Their faces shine with the determination of hard work – they bite their lips (again, those which you'll never taste) when they can't remember who ordered what, blink their eyes, and with a shrug, smile.

They wear lipstick the exact same color of their already rouge lips and leave imprints of them taking swigs off the bartender's nearly empty bottles, on the bottle's own pucker. Or they'll steal a hit off the sous-chef's cigarette. They flutter their eyes at the manager when he comes by clapping his hands and his stern tongue chirping out, constantly, *"plus vite, plus vite!"*

They check up on you asking if all's well, either pretending to care or incapable of masked pretense so you are never sure of the sincerity of their insincerities. Their hands are clean, nails manicured, and stockings dark and tight; they understand that part of the menu includes a glance their way (desire translated into a gratuitous tip).

They let you know by a look or by escorting you to the door on your way out that your tip was either fair, too little, or ample. As you go, they return your glances into a recognition, they size you up, and perhaps for a moment wonder who you are, as they wipe their forearms with a clean white towel, delicate hand on delicate clavicle, smiling, licking their teeth as they wave bye-bye to their clientele who by now are feeling the pang of another kind: goodbye, *bonsoir, bonne soirée.*

MARSEILLE, GATEWAY TO THE ORIENT, 1869, PIERRE PUVIS DE CHAVANNES

It hangs in the Palais Longchamps Musée d'Art on the wall of one of its two grand staircases. It is a gigantic canvas rendering of an imaginative and veritable history. In the background, the distinctive topography is portrayed in jutting, angular accuracy right down to the watercolor-esque washes of garrigue clinging to white hills. Notre Dame de la Garde, the phallus of Fort St. Jean, and the Cathédrale de la Major dominate the suggestion of the city's skyline, so many obelisks cut off at their points.

The sailing vessels of the foreground resemble clipper ships coming to port. The scene the painting paints occurs on the deck of one such ship bedecked with a cast of oriental caricature: exotically robed Turks, Moorish deckhands (one holding a white star and crescented flag), turbaned servants, what looks like a sailing Jew consulting a secret text. Persian rugs are rolled and unrolled (always an expensive cargo) on which a djellaba-ed woman holds a blond-haired cherub who is grasping a yellow fruit in a Madonna with child motif. A speckled doe rests with what may be the woman's young daughter.

Indians, Sephardim, Tajiks, Hazaras, Druzes, Fellahins, Armenians, Lurs are all suggested by the odd collection of men in distinctly non-European dress. Orientalism at its most blatant: a catalogue of portraiture as the "other".

The immediate foreground features three men of fair complexion — two blonds and one white-haired, mustachio-ed old man of the sea. They appear to be deckhands or Nordic pirates, these hardworking descendants of Vikings. The sea is a realistic turquoise a shade brighter than the sky torn with white crests of small, windblown waves.

In written or pictorial representations of this eastward-looking port, most are aglow in the myth of the orient. Among the silk-wrapped swarthy types there's always a reference to their opposite: a wandering German or Swede, or an Irishman out of his gloomy element. In reality the stark contrast of Marseille as a real city is not so apparent: it's a blend of peoples and colors whose difference in origins, the closer one looks, compares, attempts to differentiate, becomes incredibly difficult to discern. What is apparent is that, compared to Americans, the true-life denizens of the port city are well-kept physically, better dressed, and are assembled into portraiture.

Outside the museum, crowds throng to its grounds on a Saturday afternoon, sharing localities of gossip and small talk, while children chase each other, enacting communally what is everyone's right: the rites of spring.

OF ORIGIN AND MYTH

Between the 7th and 6th Centuries BC, the
Phoenicians . . . after consultation with the gods,
made up an expedition of men and women, taking
with them tools, plants and everything needed to
found a colony. They set off under the command of
Simos and Protis. The expedition landed at Ephesus,
where the oracle had ordered it to halt, so that Diana
could show them who was to lead them. There, a
supernatural phenomenon occurred: a famous
priestess called Aristarché saw the goddess in a
dream. On her instructions she took one of the
statues of Diana and a piece of the sacred fire and
went aboard the Phoenicians' boat so that she could
set up the worship of Diana in the new colony. Thus
both spiritual and temporal needs were provided for
and the boat set sail towards Gaul. They landed in the
Bay of Lacydon. Impressed by the suitability of the
place the immigrants wanted to settle there. To do so,
they needed permission from the King of the
Ségobriges who ruled the country. Protis was
commissioned to negotiate a treaty of alliance with
him. On that very day the old King, Mann, Nann, or
Cenomann was to give his daughter in marriage.
Protis was invited to the banquet where the other

suitors had gathered. At the end of the meal tradition
decreed that the young girl should offer a bowl of
water to the young man of her choice. It so happened
that Gyptis, struck by Protis' beauty handed him the
bowl. The old King Mann saw this as a divine
command to give the strangers a favourable welcome.
Accordingly he gave the land the Phoenicians
requested to his daughter as her dowry.
Thus Massala was founded.

Justin, Cornelius Nepos, & Eutropius. J.
Selby Watson, London: H.G. Bohn, 1853

Marseille, child of a woman's desire, as reflected in the incarnation of the golden Mary who watches over her city. Even now, womanhood is worshipped, put on such lofty pedestals, while at the same time they aren't treated equally. Femininity is however respected, ogled, sought after, and prized. Mothers are responsible for their sons until the lads are well into their forties. Women are nearly exclusively the household's chef, they also do the shopping as the gourmands that they are. As heads of this management of nutritional well-being, they rule the social hierarchy of any family and/or social gatherings. They may offer their mute opinions of financial and administrative matter.

Muses, however, are not practical stewards, and the men grant women a theater of power and sway while they are likely to usurp them whenever possible. Much hasn't changed since days gone by. The forecast for feminism in France for the upcoming millennium: nil.

GOÛTEZ!

I have just had lunch – vin blanc and
grilled sardines and carottes à la crème
and saucisses pommes parmentier and oranges.
One must never drink vin rouge in the Midi,
on m'a dit.

Katherine Mansfield, Letters

No matter the good, no matter the bad, one thing about life in France, magnified in the region of Provence, is the freedom one has of never having to plan a meal. Incredible food simply appears. There's never a need for turkey or gargantuan seventy-two ounce steaks or production lines of hot dogs and plops of charred meat patties. It is absolutely a fact that no one, not even one person, would or could ever desire or entertain such an errant thought as "microwave cooking".

Breakfast: café au lait in a handle-less bowl that is of small cereal bowl dimensions. The milk must be heated in a pan on a gas burner. The breakfast *pâtisserie* might be as simple as an untranslatable buttery croissant or a *tarte aux abricots* or another of the choices many bakeries have to tempt you with fresh every morning. Why the city architectures itself into a conglomeration of residences built above stores below: for the ability to descend a few flights of stairs into the odor of baking dough. The morning perfumes one with a hunger for life.

Lunch: might be as simple as *saucisson* and cheese with a boiled artichoke whose meat will be scraped off its hard leaves by the teeth just prior to dipping them into a spicy mustard/olive oil sauce. Perhaps some leftover *daube* – an onion, carrot, tomato, garlic, orange zest, beef, stew marinated in red wine. Or a sandwich from a vendor: *merguez frites* (heavy on the harissa), or *poulet aux poivrons* (chicken with red peppers); a *bandolais* (ground beef, onions, feta cheese, tomatoes, lettuce and really any other condiment desired). These sandwiches sunk into a one and a half foot long baguette and French fries are thrown in, actually put into the sandwich, to boot. Lunch that takes you to dinner.

Dinner: begins always with a bottle of red wine that should be sipped while preparing the meal. An olive oil, real Dijon mustard, and garlic dressing (diced red onions for a hint of extra flavor) reserved exclusively for a Medusa-like head of lettuce called *pissenlit* that is as bitter as its name for dandelion leaves indicates. To be accompanied by a few of the over five hundred kinds of cheeses available at the grocery store and a *pissaladière:* an onion tart resembling a small pizza, with black olives and a foundation/sauce of anchovy paste.

Dinner ends with one or two empty wine bottles. Dessert is fresh fruit. Knowing that there will be three such meals the next day!

PETALS ON A
WET, BLACK BOUGH

The car's interior is an odd, sickly orange. The seats are made of plastic that is a queasy shade of brown. Maybe these colors are made to represent what one should feel like while participating in public transportation. Perhaps they are a badly judged vibrancy meant to trick passengers into thinking they aren't meters deep into the rat-infested underground where cockroaches reign.

What does terrifyingly occur quite regularly is a shut down on the Marseille metro. The power cuts off. The train doesn't move. The lights go out. Darkness prevails. Then a generator turns on and dimly lights up the situation. For minutes at a time people are trapped in a coffin in which they get to know each other by scent and observe something very private and seductive: individual breaking points of anger. Eventually, the lights come on full tilt. The metro proceeds. People are late for wherever they're going, but at least they're going again.

Metrogoers are dressed for going out and about and remain tightly composed along their trips. In a place where streets erupt in garrulousness, car horn blares, deftly flung insults, the metro people are a strangely composed breed.

Curiously, they look at each other but indirectly so, through the mirror quality reflections of the interior lit glass. Sometimes chit chat staccatos the silence graciously. Sometimes whole histories or stories are told among friends or mere acquaintances as if the entire ensemble of randomly collected people cannot hear.

Is their disinterest (faux) and composure (vrai) dictated by the impersonal nature, and bad decor, of public transportation? No way of knowing except for watching their sculpted faces. In silence. Trying not to express yours.

NOT PROVENCE

But one goes to Marseilles, which is the second city of France and one of the first in Europe, for every other reason in the world than to study domestic architecture, so that no-one need miss those antiques. And the sun will always shine down on the Canebière with such vividness that it is all one whether the windows before which you pass in that famous boulevard are made of broad plate-glass or bottle-end lozenges; the cafés beneath their awnings will always buzz with rich, garlic gossip and shouted confidences whether the roadways be filled with Roman chariots or aeroplanes. The rich tang of the boastings of Marius and Olive will issue from whatever windows; the Spaniards will loll on the sunlit steps of the churches, the Catalans mend their nets on the cobbles beside the Old Port and the unending babel of sailors of whatever Mediterranean, Negroid, Levantine, Visigothic or even Scandinavian descent will for ever flow about the vast quays. For whatever Marseilles is she is not Provence. She remains perpetually a Levantine, Negroid-Semitic colony, pullulating on the edge of a scarcely habitable marsh.

Ford Maddox Ford, Provence.

Having reached its furthest most peripheries, we can only travel back to the city whose caustic traffic, occasionally inverse polluted air, and wildness of everyday spirit caused us to flee. We leave to return because it is known that however raucous and imperfect Marseille is, it is seductively livable. Nature is to be experienced but a developed mind needs other minds. It's good to return, to be among such exciting contrast: different people different days, different places, unlike the homogeneity of America where what is desired is ten million outposts selling the exact same thing. Marseille, a city defined by diversity, is spice alive.

Where else can one be where the nightly falling of the sun is extinguished by orange roof tiles, hills that resist names that blend as artful as logos from the merging metropolis into an undeniably Provençal landscape, rising from the compass point of Mt. Cyril to geometrically drop in the plane of the sea? Where restaurant owners recognize your face as you walk the city's hurried streets, chasing you down to speak of the menu of the day, inviting you to lunch, while chiding you ever so subtly for your recent absence from the fine dining of a table always reserved for you. Where there are women dressed in the most garish house dresses ever stitched together by Eastern European garment workers buying fresh fish at the port and yelling and cursing and waving their hands in a sign language that conveys this message: put up or shut up. Where slightly younger or older versions of those same women shopping in supermarkets wear the latest from Paris, who afterwards will be seen on the beach having discarded most of their fine garments leaving one to consider and reconsider their, and your own, marital status. Where men don all types of old stained, twilled hats in styles that never range too far from that of the beret (though no one wears berets!) as they spend the afternoons doing as little as possible, which is both a privilege and an art form, as they watch those women as if the men were somehow attractive enough to even have the right to desire such ladies. Where there are stands selling bulbous strings of garlic hung under a makeshift steel-poled tent, cloves upon cloves upon cloves stacked on wooden crates, peeling from their skins to leave the ground around confetti-ed with their meaty, hearty, tangy smell, as the garlic vendor rests his frame on the curb reading yesterday's paper that someone didn't care enough to throw away. Where small fishing boats bee-lining in the distance of blue margin trailing eager flocks of hungry gulls who queue for scraps of fish innards, flying like white surrender flags of hunger attached to nothing. Where houseboats gently bob and sway in the port, each a private version of Venice, boxes of sub-cities empty with napping inhabitants. Where fortresses encage strata of square, interconnected, attached buildings adorned with spires or secret cabin-type lofts with what must be incredible views (you will never see them), fortresses that protect against the myth of modern-day invaders but command visual respect from the populace still interested in history, military, their timeworn walls so cracked and in ill repair that offshoots of trees have begun to sprout within their ancient furrows. Where there are dwellings so near the sea they look like the coastal rock bed they are built into so that limestone lip hardened over the sea looks as if it has been carved into geometries of houses Greeks would kill to live in: mathematics of habitation above water. Where the city's bustling ever-expanding, regenerating center has enough heart to conceal a tiny village port of Vallon des Auffes – a depression in which the houses are so close together everyone there is a part of everyone else's family. Where the alleys are so thin and narrow its hard to view the sky and the proximity of co-habitations doesn't allow one to participate in overly vocal celebrations of life's most intimate intimacies: arguments, television viewing, siren songs of sex. Where the islands close enough to be continually seen give free lessons in climatology and geology as they shapeshift under the day's wardrobe change of sunlight, where only the aerials topping them like established colonies on meteors allow any claim as to their presumed heights. Where flowers perpetually bloom and the opportunity of a garden, in a crowded, limited city space (two thousand and six hundred years of gardening!), is never taken for granted. Where there is a complete lack of yard or home ornamentation of the kitsch variety – no lawn deer, no ring bearing houseboys. Where the sea can become so angry that it spits on cars traveling on the Corniche and its waves crushed by the force of wind and stone create instantaneous low-level cloudshows that leave you with the souvenir of wet salty clothes. Where the coast appears to be a loose conglomeration of isolated islands that by a trick of sight and perspective and distance seem to line up into a sparsely populated isthmus. Where forgotten alleys are overgrown in ivies and poppies and weeds trying their best to hide the thruways as they do their best to conceal shortcuts in mime-plays of what it is like to be mountain lupine. Where sad, dark-skinned boys will try to sell you stolen cigarettes or offer to wash the windows of your car even if you are walking along with no such technology. Where stacks and stacks of anonymous, indistinguishable high-rises hide legions of people who rarely peek from their prisons of windows and clothesline but at exactly six o'clock p.m. create a powerful brew of simple but exquisite dinners drenched in the juices of lamb, onions, garlic, butter, clouds of saffron and walls crying with the steam of pots of couscous, oregano mists hanging invisibly in the air. Where the ruins of Greek docks are fenced in by an iron gate holding back bushes that have never been trimmed, making perfect hideouts for stray cats who mark their territories with a urine so sour it makes you sneeze, ruins sunken just east into the Old Port's mouth and absconded by churches, block apartments, the Bourse, so whoever comes upon them does so accidentally. Where the entrance to a city's main boulevard is announced by a carousel's plaintive organ croon and the children who ride it first see and think that the *centre ville* is a place that spins round and round them. Where the omniscient Moorish dome of the Vieille Charité invites you to walk to it through the poor immigrant quarter it presides over, into its Naples of sorts where clothes and undergarments brazenly soak up wind and sun from their stiff poses on tethered lines above streets Nazis once blew up. Where the Panier feels as downtrodden as the dying light in the few shops pretending to make enough money to survive and in the shadow of the ancient hospice that now houses museums and shops and a restaurant that those who live around could never afford but who regularly visit its sumptuous, shady Andalusian court. The Vieille Charité whose open-air halls and corridors are walked to view the city from above and within, on a hill where there was once a line of windmills. Where now on the canvas of sight the ever-present sea is blocked by modernity's ugly progress and looking out into the uncountable prisons of residencies, one feels a prisoner in a foreign land, a man or woman in a concrete mask. Where ancient crypts emit scents that even strong incense cannot cover. Where shops in the garment district inhabit the sites of former public baths, each dressing room where an ancestor stood naked and alone, clothes stores that sell not only garments but artwork, decorative craftwork made of bronze and tin created by artisans of African kingdoms. Where parks are used to take pleasures in publicly, especially kissing, newspaper reading, playing, taking meals, singing out loud, discussing life, and what's best – staying in the park all day long doing nothing. Where sunsets light upon exquisite and damned architecture with a memento of brilliance, signaling their desire to be anything other than zoos of participatory ennui. Where the omnipresent mountains beyond seem to be drying fish with white and green scales lying on their sides, taking their last breaths as they dream of a sleep that will kill them. Where roofs and facades combine to be beds of rock from which bricks are mined then arrayed with cheap crosses of television antennae as pigeons in rookeries wonder what these perfect perches for themselves were put there for. Where magazine stands flash pictures of nude bodies for anyone at any time to see with the purchase of one's guilt the only fee. Where *boules* is played or cards, or shopping done throughout the day because there isn't much else to be done. Where people crossing streets rarely ever pay attention to the flow of traffic and drivers wait patiently to proceed without getting angry! Where cheap supermarkets, mini-markets and Baze-like grocery stores play scary intercom music and are filled with hot, tired, desperate shoppers that do not take kindly to lines at 5:30pm. Where anything wanted, needed, desired, hankered for, plus a thousand of those selfsame things exist that you never even knew about until you went out looking for them in the city that lights itself green at night and then becomes busier, louder, more enjoyable to be lost in. Where the modern port extends like an erector set village seen from the shores where older buildings, separated coagulated boxes tempted you to find where the gigantic floating cities of cargo ships come in at but your adventure was stopped almost immediately by a special police force who patrol the riches waiting to be transported from non-descript steel sarcophagi. Where a cathedral with a golden saint watches over all as if religion still mattered. Where ferries like fallen floating skyscrapers skirt to and fro in between their intercontinental voyages. Where no matter how many streets are walked and bistros known and people met and menus studied, the vast seeping cosmopolitan Mediterraneanness never lets you or anyone else feel as if it is a place to rest forever. It's a moveable voyage of a feast that at once is an ever-changing port fluxing in overlapping cultures and for this entity we call Western culture the closest eutopia that we might call "home".

ACKNOWLEDGMENTS

With thanks to the keen mind of Crizia Bonifaci.

Excerpts have appeared in *The Iowa Review* and *Colorado Review, Northern Ohio Review, Palimpsest, Glassworks, Hotel Amerika*

View from a Solitary Location; Landscape, with White Deserts; and *A Walk in the Calanques* appeared in an adumbrated form in *Connecticut Review*

Mazargues appeared in *Referential Magaine*

Archipelago Inconnu, Cahokia of Our Own appeared in *Cahaba River Literary Journal*, 2015

In Merovingia appeared in *Serving House Books Paris Anthology*, 2015

Marseille in Bites appeared in *Annapurna Magazine*, 2013

ABOUT THE AUTHOR

Philip Kobylarz is an itinerant teacher of the language arts and writer of fiction, poetry, book reviews, and essays. He has been a journalist, a film critic, a veterinarian's assistant, a deliverer of furniture, and an ascetic.

Philip's work appears in such publications as *Paris Review*, *Poetry*, *The Best American Poetry* series, *Massachusetts Review*, and *Lalitamba*. His first book, Zen-inspired poems concerning life in the south of France, is entitled *rues*. His second book, short stories and a novella, is titled *Now Leaving Nowheresville*. An experimental, encyclopedic work, *A Miscellany of Diverse Things*, was published by Brooklyn's *Lit Riot Press* in 2017.

He lives ever so temporarily in the East Bay of San Francisco.

www.ingramcontent.com/pod-product-compliance
Lightning Source LLC
Chambersburg PA
CBHW031947080426

42735CB00007B/299